The Basics of the Christian Faith

DISCIPLESHIP COURSE

The Basics of the Christian Faith
Copyright © 2023 by Truth For Life
P. O. Box 398000 Cleveland, OH 44139

All Scripture quotations, unless otherwise indicated, are taken from *The Holy Bible, English Standard Version*. Copyright © 2001 by Crossway Bibles, a division of Good News Publishers. Used by permission. All rights reserved.

Welcome, Leader

We're so glad you've chosen to share, study, and discuss *The Basics of the Christian Faith* with a friend who is a new believer or is interested in learning more about Christianity. While most people are familiar with the word *disciple*, they may not fully understand what it means to *be* a disciple or to *make* disciples, as Jesus commanded His followers in Matthew 28:19. And so we hope you find that this study helps you explain and teach how being a disciple of Jesus leads to eternal life.

As you and your friend listen to the thirteen messages that form the basis of this study then meet to discuss answers to the questions associated with each lesson, you'll have the amazing privilege of demonstrating what it looks like to be a committed follower—*a disciple*—of Jesus Christ.

Prayer will be helpful throughout the process. Alistair often reminds us that people are brought to saving faith only when *God's Spirit does God's work through God's Word*. So pray for God to use all that will be learned to reveal His truth to your friend.

USING THIS GUIDE TO

Share Your Faith with a Friend

These lessons will help you and your friend grow in your knowledge of Christ and encourage one another's faith (Rom. 1:12). Each session includes three learning phases to complete independently before meeting in person. The purpose of this study guide is to provide you with an opportunity to share your faith not just through personal testimony but also by considering the essential truths that God has revealed in His Word. Your role as the leader is to grasp the content, facilitate discussion, provide biblical answers and explanations, and—most importantly—exemplify God's love.

Tips for before You Begin

- Consider having an informal meeting or conversation to talk about your friend's
    1. goals and expectations,
    2. current understanding of Christianity, and
    3. faith background.

- Familiarize yourself with the study's structure.

- Tap the **+** on the *The Basics of the Christian Faith* series page to add it to "My Library" for easy tracking and access while you're online or using the Truth For Life mobile app.

- Do you prefer listening or reading—or both? All of the messages have both the audio and the transcripts available for free.

- Pray.

WHAT YOU'LL BE

Helping Your Friend Learn

"

We must endeavor to understand the first principles of Christian doctrine and to bring those principles to bear on every aspect of our lives, lest we be swept away.

ALISTAIR BEGG

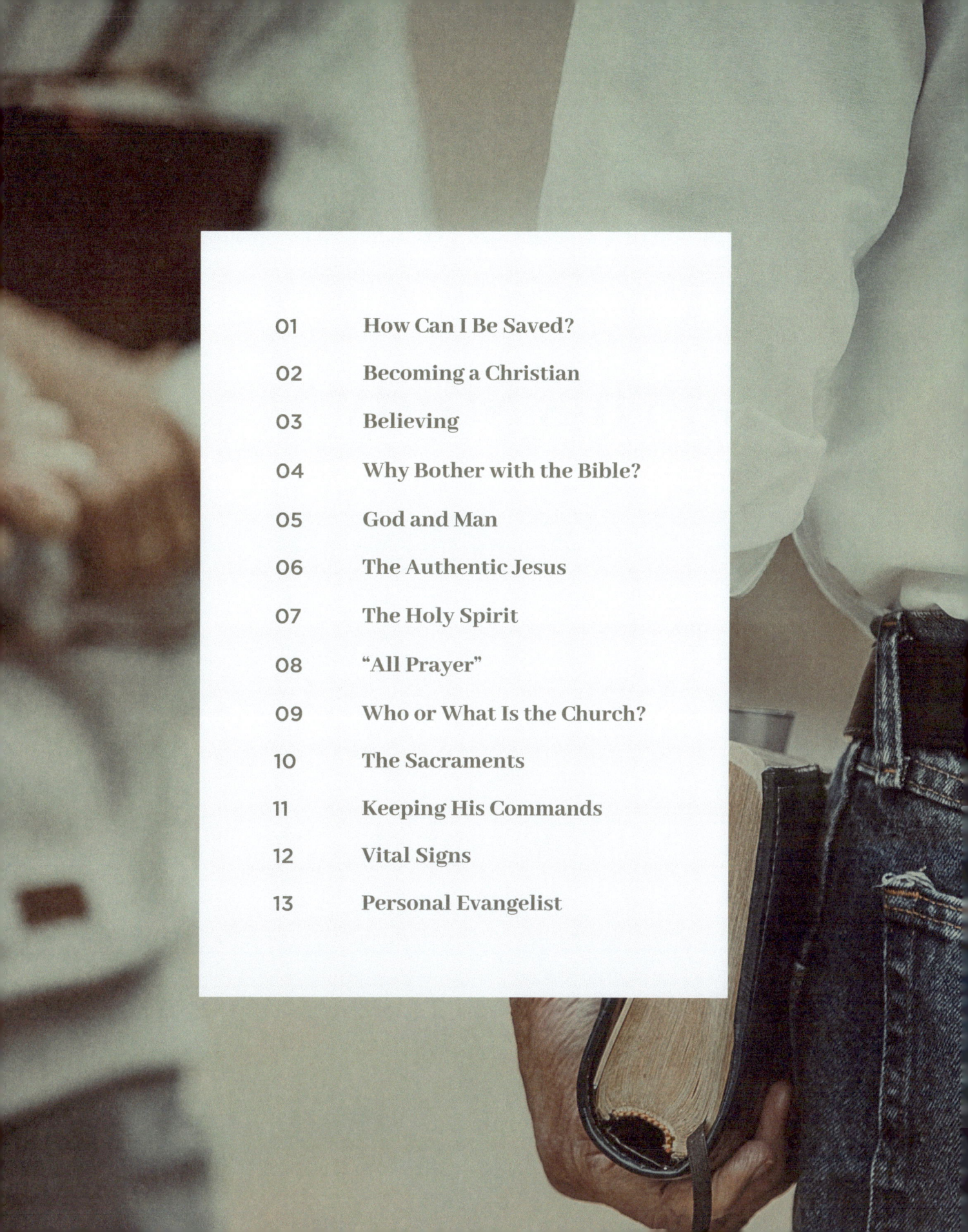

01	How Can I Be Saved?
02	Becoming a Christian
03	Believing
04	Why Bother with the Bible?
05	God and Man
06	The Authentic Jesus
07	The Holy Spirit
08	"All Prayer"
09	Who or What Is the Church?
10	The Sacraments
11	Keeping His Commands
12	Vital Signs
13	Personal Evangelist

HOW TO

Use This Study

This study is designed to pair independent listening to sermons by Alistair Begg with in-person discussion between you and a friend whom you will lead through each lesson. You'll have the most success when you complete each of the three learning phases on your own then meet together to discuss your responses and answer any questions your friend may have. When you meet, you may want to spend additional time on particular sessions, revisit questions that came up in earlier meetings, or otherwise use the format in a flexible way. *You* are the one who knows your study partner, so make the study work toward your goals!

LET'S

Get Started!

EACH LESSON HAS

Three Learning Phases

Each session in this study corresponds to a sermon from Alistair Begg and follows a three-part outline before concluding with a reflective **Praise & Prayer** section. **Additional Resources** are suggested for diving deeper into related content.

Getting Started | ⏳ 5 – 10 mins.

You'll begin by reading a key passage of Scripture and answering a few questions before listening to the lesson's message. When you meet, you should reread the passage together and be prepared to discuss your responses.

Listen & Learn | ⏳ 30 – 40 mins.

In this phase, you'll read or listen to the lesson's message. (A brief summary of each message is provided.) As you do so, you should take notes, fill in the blanks,* read the definitions, and answer the corresponding questions.* You might also want to use the additional space provided to take notes on key points you want to emphasize when you discuss the sermon with your friend.

Going Deeper | ⏳ 10 – 15 mins.

The questions in this phase are meant to help your friend fully process and apply the main ideas that were taught. You should be prepared to discuss your answers and other questions that your friend might have.

*An answer key can be found at the back of this guide.

SESSION

01

How Can I Be Saved?

> "
>
> There is only one way to be saved, and that is by doing two things: by turning *from* my sin and turning *to* Christ as the Savior from the sin that I admit.
>
> ALISTAIR BEGG

Note to Leader: If you haven't heard your friend profess faith or you have questions and concerns about his or her standing with God, pray that the Spirit will give you love, boldness, and the right words to share His truth.

SESSION 01

How Can I Be Saved?

Getting Started

01.   What do you think of when you hear the word *salvation*?

02.   What does it mean for Jesus to be someone's Savior?

📖 **Read Ephesians 2:1–10 and answer the questions below.**

01. What do you learn about mankind from verses 1–3?

02. What are salvation's source and purpose according to verses 4–7?

03. According to verses 8–10, how does God save us?

Listen to "How Can I Be Saved?"
Scan the QR code or visit tfl.org/christian-faith.

SESSION 01

How Can I Be Saved?

Listen & Learn

Conditions of entry are important—especially concerning the kingdom of heaven. The Bible is clear about the problem of humanity in our natural state: we are dead, blind, and enslaved due to sin. The solution God offers is salvation through Jesus Christ. But how can we be saved? The Bible teaches that salvation comes from turning away from sin toward Christ as Savior.

Salvation is an essential prerequisite to discipleship. Before we can follow Jesus, we must know Him as our Savior. The purpose of this lesson is to help you grasp how God works to bring His people to salvation.

Key Terms

repentance

the act of turning *from sin* with godly remorse and to *God* out of love and reverence for Him

salvation

the reality of being rescued from sin's penalty upon one's genuine profession of faith, from sin's power through the enabling of God's Spirit, and from sin's presence upon entering Christ's company

Fill in the Blank

01. "Salvation is not _____ works, but it is _____ works."

02. "There is only one way to be saved, and that is by doing two things: by turning from ____ _____ and turning to _____."

03. "There are two places that sin is punished: sin is punished in _____, and sin is punished at _____. And the message of the Gospel is '_____ in Jesus Christ today as your _____ and _____, or face Him then as your rightful _____.'"

PAGE 12 THE BASICS OF THE CHRISTIAN FAITH

Short Answer

01. How does Alistair describe the meaning of the Greek word for *repentance*?

02. Alistair asks, "If I promise simply to do better, won't God save me?" What is the biblical answer to that question?

Notes

Additional notes on page 18

SESSION 01

How Can I Be Saved?

Going Deeper

01. In the sermon, Alistair asks, "Have you ever repented? Have you ever reached a day in your life where the claims of Christ came to you with such clarity that you said, 'This is something I must do; I'm on the wrong road'?" If your answer is "Yes," how has your life since changed? If "No," what is holding you back?

02.   Alistair also asks, "If you have understood the claims of Christ, if you have understood the message, what prevents you, right now, today, from bowing your head and, in your own silent prayer to Christ, acknowledging that you need Him, turning your life over to Him, and walking out in friendship with Him?" Whether you have believed in Jesus for five minutes or for many years, take a moment to pause and acknowledge your constant need of Him.

03.   Who in your life needs to hear this message of salvation? Write down at least one name and a brief prayer for that individual.

Notes Continued...

SESSION 01
How Can I Be Saved?

Praise & Prayer

*Amazing grace—how sweet the sound—
That saved a wretch like me!
I once was lost but now am found,
Was blind but now I see.*

*'Twas grace that taught my heart to fear,
And grace my fears relieved;
How precious did that grace appear
The hour I first believed!*

"Amazing Grace"
John Newton

*L*ord *Jesus Christ, I have long been so foolish. Give me Your wisdom to see and to follow Your truth. I am so full of guilt and have no peace apart from You, but now I see that You have died to bring forgiveness and the assurance of pardon. I trust You to be my Savior, and by Your grace, I turn away from my sin. Lord, apart from You I am weak and ruled by sin. Give me Your power, and rule in my heart. Set me free, and take charge of my whole life.*

Amen

SESSION 01
How Can I Be Saved?

Additional Resources

Online Resources
Sermons, articles, and devotions can be found by scanning the QR code or by visiting tfl.org/christian-faith-list.

Sermons by Alistair
- "The Nature and Necessity of Repentance"
- "Divine Righteousness Applied"

Articles & Devotions
- "What Is the Gospel?"
- "To the Almost Christian"
- "Now Is the Time"

Recommended Books
- *Basic Christianity* by John Stott
- *What Is the Gospel?* by Greg Gilbert

SESSION

02

Becoming a Christian

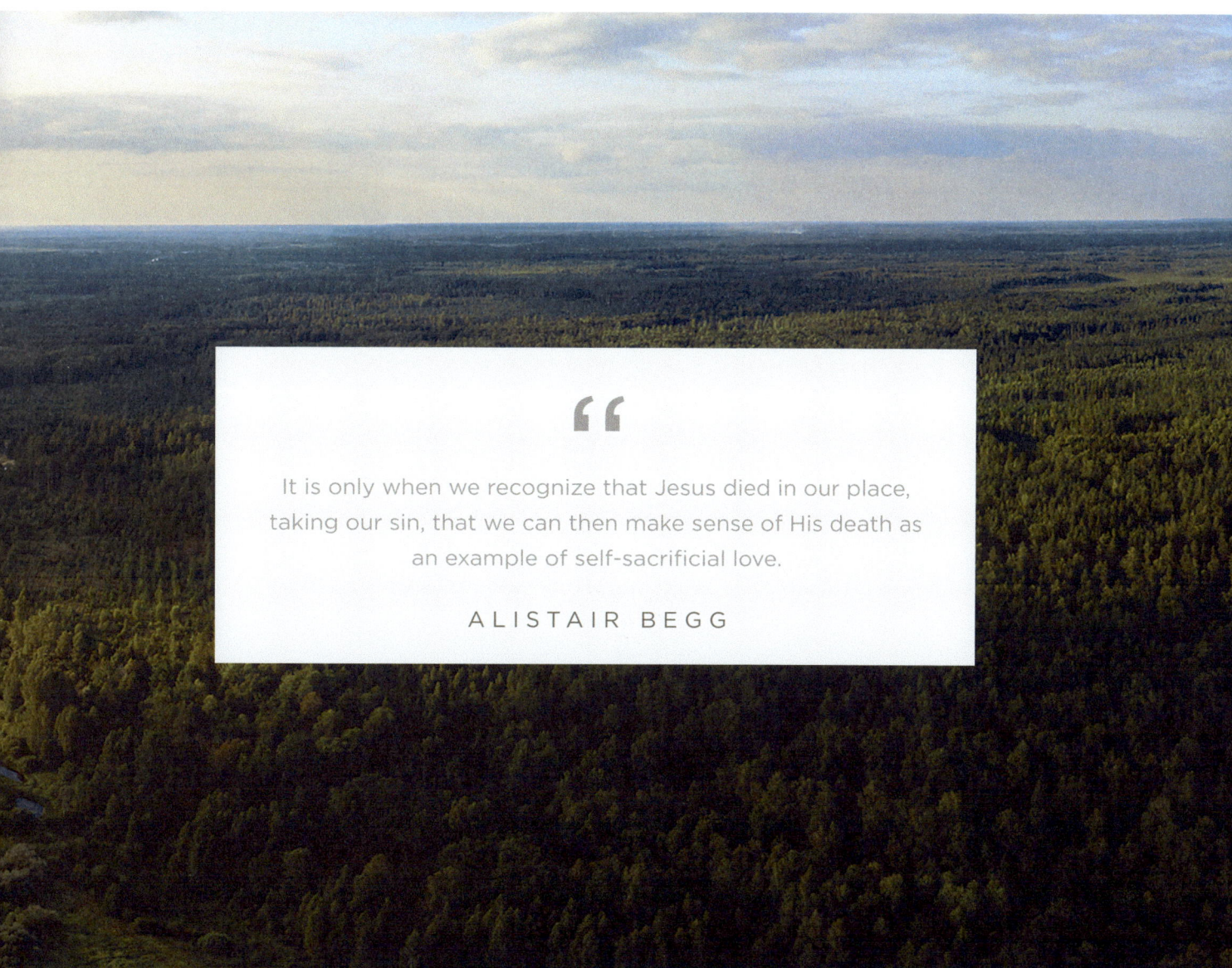

> "
>
> It is only when we recognize that Jesus died in our place, taking our sin, that we can then make sense of His death as an example of self-sacrificial love.
>
> ALISTAIR BEGG

Note to Leader: This session serves as a reminder that *all* of us need to be washed clean. Pray that you will demonstrate humility by acknowledging your own constant need of God's grace.

SESSION 02

Becoming a Christian

Getting Started

01. In your own words, explain how someone becomes a Christian.

02. What Bible verses support your answer to the previous question?

📖 Read Luke 5:12–13 and answer the questions below.

01. What do you learn about the character and identity of Jesus from these verses?

02. How is the leper a model of faith?

SESSION 02 • BECOMING A CHRISTIAN   PAGE 21

Listen to "Becoming a Christian"
Scan the QR code or visit tfl.org/christian-faith.

SESSION 02
Becoming a Christian

Listen & Learn

When Jesus visited a town in Galilee, He healed a man hopelessly consumed by leprosy with His compassionate touch. Like leprosy, sin corrupts the souls of men and women completely, making us alienated from God, hopeless to save ourselves, and in desperate need of rescue. But there is hope! Jesus died for sin to meet our greatest need. In response, we are called to cast ourselves on His mercy.

Key Terms
alienation the state and experience of being separated and estranged
leprosy in biblical times, a word that described various skin ailments that typically resulted in the affected individual's alienation from society and its norms

As disciples of Christ, we must also know how to help others become Christians. The purpose of this lesson is to clarify how one begins new life as a believer so that you may be able to clearly articulate to others how they might do so themselves.

Fill in the Blank

01. "Jesus makes it clear by the time He steps on the stage of history, referencing the historicity of Adam and Eve, that the death that entered into the world was the _____ death, closing down the _____ between a holy God and His creation, bringing _____ into that picture, bringing bondage into people's lives, bringing conflict into their circumstances."

02. "Every one of us is _____ with an inherent _____ to sin, every one of us a _____ in the same sinking ship with everybody else. And every day we are confronted by the ravaging nature of our condition."

03. "Sin is not an _____ problem; it is a _____ problem."

PAGE 22 — THE BASICS OF THE CHRISTIAN FAITH

Short Answer

01.   How is leprosy a picture of our sinful condition?

02.   What are the three elements of saving faith?

Notes

Additional notes on page 28

SESSION 02
Becoming a Christian

Going Deeper

01. What are some reasons that you might find it difficult to believe not only that Jesus is compassionate but also that He actually desires to cleanse you from your sin?

02. If you want to know whether the miracle of salvation has occurred in your life, Alistair recommends that you consider these questions: Are you beginning to see that you've done wrong and that God is rightly angry with you? Are you beginning to sense that Jesus has been sent by God the Father to bring you forgiveness? How has God's offer of salvation changed your life?

Notes Continued...

SESSION 02
Becoming a Christian

Praise & Prayer

*And can it be that I should gain
An interest in the Savior's blood?
Died He for me, who caused His pain?
For me, who Him to death pursued?
Amazing love! How can it be
That Thou, my God, shouldst die for me?*

**"And Can It Be
That I Should Gain?"**
Charles Wesley

O Lord, I admit that I am weaker and more sinful than I ever before believed, but through You I am more loved and accepted than I ever dared hope. I thank You for paying my debt, bearing my punishment, and offering me forgiveness. Help me to turn from my sin today and every day, always humbly acknowledging that You are my Savior and living for Your glory.

Amen

SESSION 02

Becoming a Christian

Additional Resources

 ## Online Resources
Sermons, articles, and devotions can be found by scanning the QR code or by visiting tfl.org/christian-faith-list.

Sermons by Alistair

- "Faith in Jesus"
- "True Freedom"

Articles & Devotions

- "The New and Better Adam"
- "What Does the Bible Teach about Becoming a Christian?"
- "What Is True Faith?"

Recommended Books

- *Mere Christianity* by C. S. Lewis
- *The Christian Life* by Sinclair B. Ferguson

SESSION

03
Believing

> "
> Only when God is pleased to take the initiative and reveal Himself may we know just what it is and why it is we believe. That happens as a result of God using His Word and as a result of God working by His Spirit.
>
> ALISTAIR BEGG

Note to Leader

Doctrinal commitment should never be so intense that we become rigid and demand too much from others or ourselves. As Alistair so often teaches, the main things are the plain things. God has made clear all that is necessary for salvation and joyful obedience.

SESSION 03

Believing

Getting Started

01. How would you define the word *doctrine*? What do you think of when you hear or read that word?

02. How do Christians know what they are supposed to believe?

📖 **Read Colossians 1:21–23 and answer the questions below.**

01. According to these verses, how are we reconciled to God and for what purpose?

02. What does Paul say we must do to remain "holy and blameless and above reproach" before God?

Listen to "Believing"
Scan the QR code or visit tfl.org/christian-faith.

02

SESSION 03
Believing

Listen & Learn

Throughout the centuries, the church has consistently maintained that believers should be firmly grounded in the essentials of the faith. In this message, Alistair draws on both history and Scripture to emphasize the necessity for every Christian to know what they believe and why they believe it. Understanding basic Christian doctrine and applying these principles to every aspect of our lives is crucial for discerning what's right and wrong and for passing on the truth to future generations.

> ### Key Terms
>
> **general revelation**
> the universal truths in the world that are sufficient to convince men and women of God's existence and to leave them "without excuse" as it relates to disobedience toward Him (see Rom. 1:18–20)
>
> **special revelation**
> the miraculous ways in which God has chosen to reveal Himself to men and women, e.g., the written Word (the Bible) and the incarnate Word (Jesus)

If you want to persevere in the faith as a Christian, basic Christian beliefs must be deeply rooted in your heart. This lesson will help you understand the importance of knowing essential Christian beliefs for yourself so that you will remain faithful to Christ and encourage others to remain faithful to Him as well.

Fill in the Blank

01. "It is impossible to go through the Letters without finding that again and again the apostles are urging upon their readers the absolute necessity of knowing _____ and _____ they believe."

02. "_____ is not the key in learning Christian doctrine. _____ is the key in learning Christian doctrine."

PAGE 32   THE BASICS OF THE CHRISTIAN FAITH

Short Answer

01. How is the Bible's veracity—its truthfulness—*ultimately* confirmed for us?

02. List at least five essential doctrines that Alistair identifies.

Notes

Additional notes on page 38

SESSION 03

Believing

Going Deeper

01. Why is it important to know what you believe and why you believe it?

02. In Alistair's list of essential doctrines, which is the hardest for you to grasp? Which is the easiest? Why?

03. Alistair mentions that the church sows the seeds of its own destruction when it gets distracted by numbers and clever methodologies for reaching unbelievers. Why is this so?

Notes Continued...

SESSION 03
Believing

Praise & Prayer

*Be Thou my wisdom
And Thou my true word,
I ever with Thee
And Thou with me, Lord,
Thou my great Father,
I Thy true son,
Thou in me dwelling
And I with Thee one.*

"Be Thou My Vision"

*F*ather, thank You that You have given me the Bible. Thank You that You've given the Holy Spirit to illumine the printed page to me and sensitize my heart to its truth. Thank You that You've given me intellect so that I may be able think rationally about things. Help me to become a man or woman of the Book. You have exalted above all things Your name and Your Word.

*L*ord Jesus, every other name is subservient to Yours. Every other shepherd points to You, the Great Shepherd. Every teacher is a learner from You, Christ, the great Teacher of Your people. It is in You, Lord Jesus Christ alone, that all my hope is found. You are everything, Jesus. May I live out that reality in the days of this coming week. For I pray in Your precious name.

Amen

SESSION 03
Believing

Additional Resources

Online Resources
Sermons, articles, and devotions can be found by scanning the QR code or by visiting tfl.org/christian-faith-list.

Sermons by Alistair

- "Theological Realism"
- "Here I Stand"

Articles & Devotions

- "From Milk to Food"
- "Five Nonessentials of the Christian Faith"

Recommended Books

- *A Little Book for New Theologians* by Kelly M. Kapic
- *A Faith to Live By* by Donald Macleod
- *A Body of Divinity* by Thomas Watson

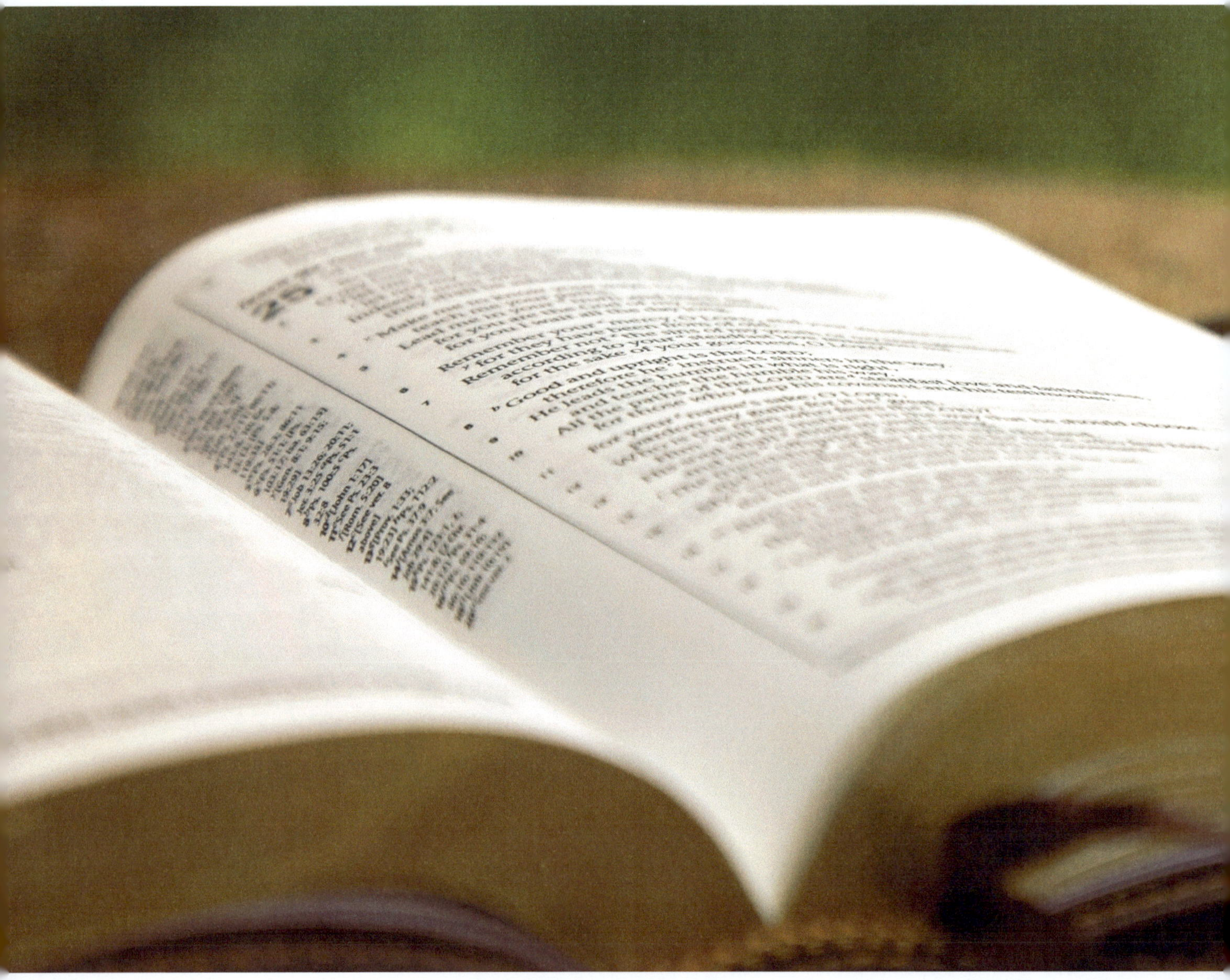

SESSION

04

Why Bother with the Bible?

> "
> The Bible is a book like no other book, inasmuch as it is a book that understands us.
>
> ALISTAIR BEGG

01

Note to Leader: Use this opportunity to make sure your friend is aware of free, helpful Bible tools such as truthforlife.org/bible, esv.org, biblehub.com, and more.

SESSION 03

Believing

Getting Started

01.   What are some facts that you know about the Bible?

02.   What is something regarding Scripture you'd like to learn more about?

📖 **Read 2 Timothy 3:14–17 and answer the questions below.**

01. Where does Scripture find its origin according to these verses?

02. What is Scripture useful for, and what does this indicate about its importance in the Christian life?

Listen to "Why Bother with the Bible?"
Scan the QR code or visit tfl.org/christian-faith.

SESSION 04

Why Bother with the Bible?

Listen & Learn

It's the best-selling book of all time: written over thousands of years by dozens of different writers, the Bible is a timeless and remarkable piece of historic literature. Is that all the Bible is, though—a classic book? Why bother with it? In answer to this question, Alistair examines 2 Timothy, teaching us that the Bible is central to all we do as Christians because it is the means through which God speaks to us.

> **Key Term**
>
> **dual authorship**
>
> the idea that the Scriptures were written (or spoken) by both God and man. As Peter reminds his readers, "no prophecy was ever produced by the will of man, but men spoke from God as they were carried along by the Holy Spirit" (2 Peter 1:21).

There is no such thing as a growing Christian who does not have a relationship with God through His Word. The purpose of this lesson is to help you learn the importance of Scripture and how to read and study it for yourself so that you may continue to grow as a disciple of Jesus.

Fill in the Blank

01. "There is a part which in the table of contents is called the _____, which goes from Genesis to Malachi, and then there is the _____, which goes from Matthew through to Revelation."

02. The Bible is "_____ books written in a variety of languages, mainly in _____ and _____, over a period of more than a thousand years, originating in places as far apart as Babylon and Rome, and penned by as many as _____ different individuals."

03. In the Old Testament, Jesus is _____; in the Gospels, He is _____; in the Acts of the Apostles, He is _____; in the Epistles, He is _____; and in the book of Revelation, He is _____.

Short Answer

01. What does Alistair say is the purpose of the Bible?

02. List the principles of biblical interpretation mentioned in the sermon.

Notes

Additional notes on page 48

SESSION 04

Why Bother with the Bible?

Going Deeper

01. What does it mean that the Scriptures are God-breathed?

02. What metaphor does the apostle Peter use to describe God's activity in the process of Scripture being written by human authors? What does this metaphor teach you about the nature of the Bible?

Notes Continued...

SESSION 04
Why Bother with the Bible?

Praise & Prayer

How firm a foundation, ye saints of the Lord,
Is laid for your faith in His excellent Word!
What more can He say than to you He hath said,
You who unto Jesus for refuge have fled?

"How Firm a Foundation"

O God, thank You that You have spoken, and as a result of that, I am enabled by Your grace to respond. Thank You for the Bible—that it is a lamp that shines on my feet, a light that opens up my path. Shine the light of Your Word into my life, so that in understanding its purpose—to make me wise to salvation—I might then be thoroughly equipped for every good work.

Amen

SESSION 04

Why Bother with the Bible?

Additional Resources

Online Resources
Sermons, articles, and devotions can be found by scanning the QR code or by visiting tfl.org/christian-faith-list.

Sermons by Alistair

- "The Bible: An Overview"
- "Why Bother with the Bible? — Part Two"
- "Why Bother with the Bible? — Part Three"

Articles & Devotions

- "The Doctrine of the Scripture"
- "Three Questions about the Bible: What Is It? Who Wrote It? How Can We Understand It?"

Recommended Books

- *The Inspiration and Authority of the Bible* by B. B. Warfield
- *The Way of Life* by Charles Hodge

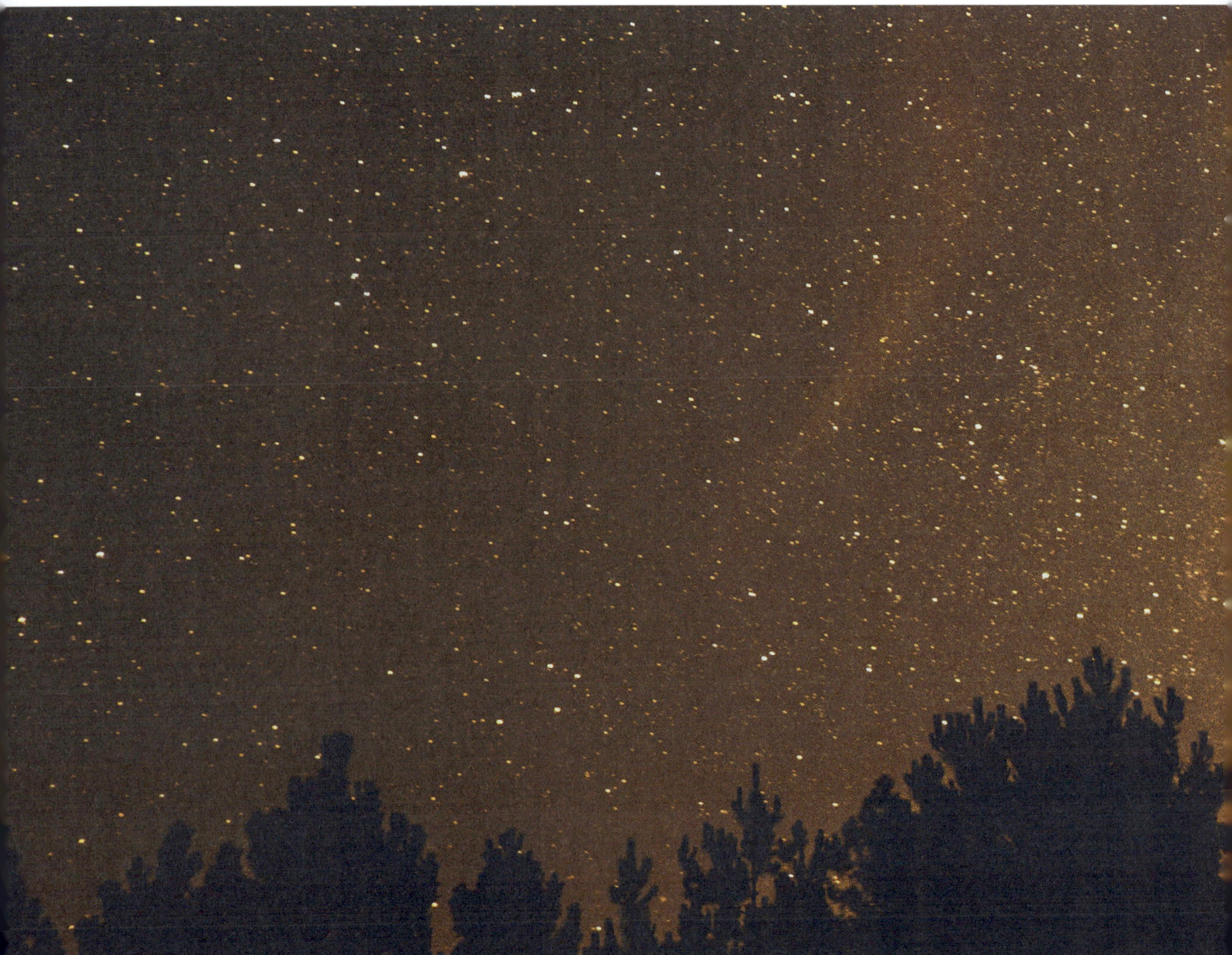

SESSION

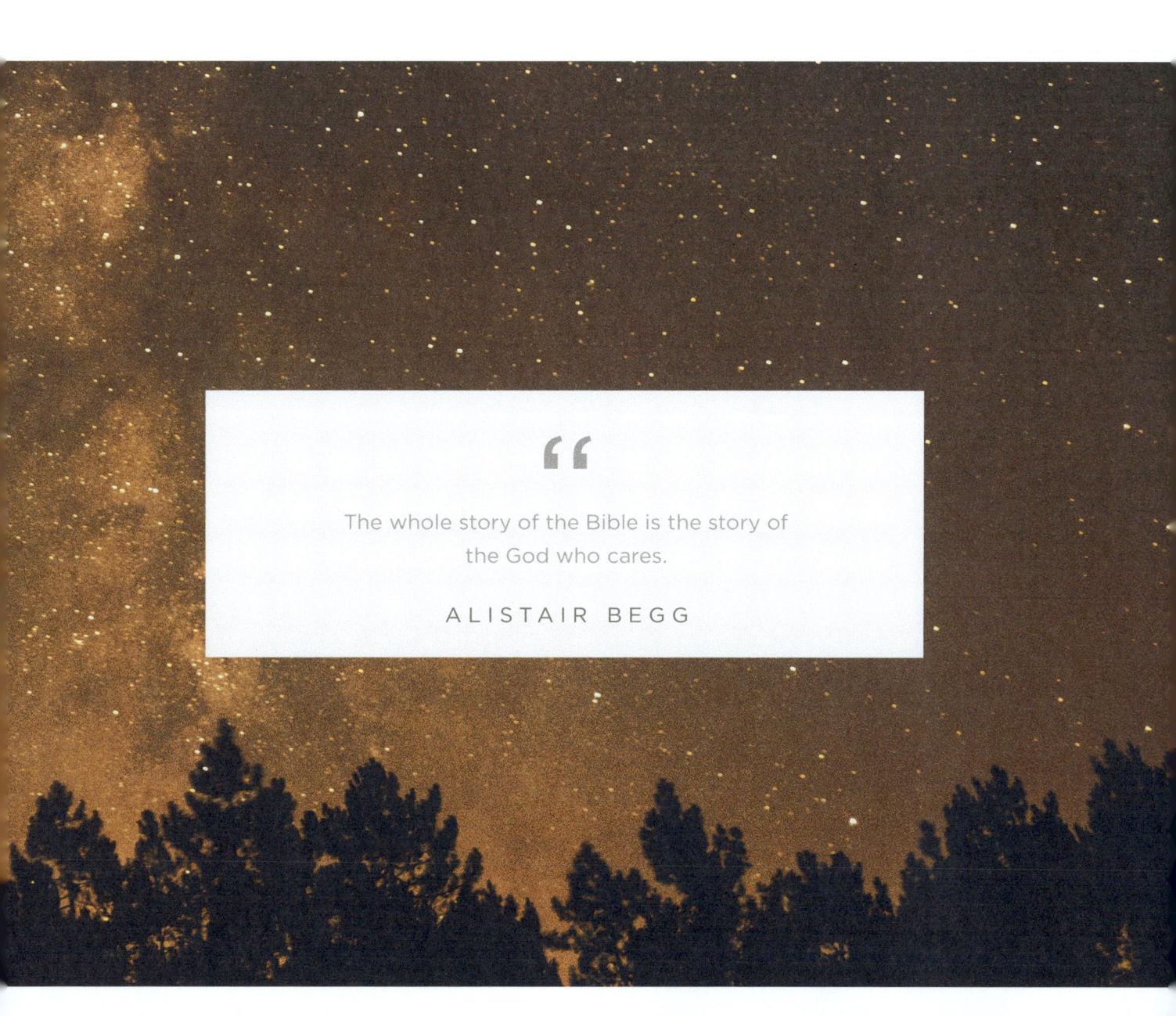

05

God and Man

> "
> The whole story of the Bible is the story of the God who cares.
>
> ALISTAIR BEGG

01

Note to Leader: It might be helpful to begin your meeting for this session by discussing Genesis 3's account of mankind's fall and its implications for all of life. (E.g., see 1 Cor. 15:21–22.)

SESSION 05

God and Man

Getting Started

01. Imagine that someone who has never heard of God asks you to describe Him. How would you do so?

02. What are some traits that set humanity apart from the rest of God's creation?

📖 **Read Psalm 8:1–9 and answer the questions below.**

01. Why does David seem surprised that God is mindful of mankind?

02. According to this psalm, what roles has God given to various parts of His creation?

02

Listen to "God and Man"
Scan the QR code or visit tfl.org/christian-faith.

SESSION 05
God and Man

Listen & Learn

Who is God? Psalm 8 proclaims that He is the Lord, the ruler of all things who created mankind in His image. Our inherent dignity, however, has been tarnished by sin. Contrasting God's greatness with humanity's frailty, Alistair demonstrates the immense care for us that God expressed through the death of His Son, Jesus. It is this God alone who reaches out to us, answering the deepest questions of our souls.

> **Key Terms**
>
> **human depravity**
> the doctrine that there is no area of our lives that is unaffected by sin, which affects our wills, minds, bodies, emotions, behavior, and more
>
> **the image of God**
> (*imago Dei*)
> humanity's nature insofar as we are made to resemble God, unlike the rest of creation

Unless we first understand God's identity, we will never make sense of our own. When we understand who God is and who we are in relation to Him, we will embrace God's design for our life all the more eagerly.

Fill in the Blank

01. "If we ask the question 'Who, then, is this God?' the first answer is that He is _____."

02. "The story of Christianity is that the _____ of the universe has stepped down into time. And indeed, He has done so because He _____."

PAGE 52 — THE BASICS OF THE CHRISTIAN FAITH

Short Answer

01. What is the source of the dignity that humans possess?

02. What are humanity's two characteristic marks according to Scripture?

03. What does Scripture teach us about our relationship to God?

04. What is the great hope for those who have been reconciled to God?

Notes

Additional notes on page 58

03

SESSION 05
God and Man

Going Deeper

01. What did you learn about God in this sermon? How do these truths about God help you to think rightly about yourself?

02. All people have dignity because they are created in the image of God, and at the same time, all people are sinners because of the fall. How should these two characteristics of humanity influence the way that you think about and relate to other people?

Notes Continued...

SESSION 05
God and Man

Praise & Prayer

*Great is Thy faithfulness, O God my Father;
There is no shadow of turning with Thee.
Thou changest not, Thy compassions, they fail not;
As Thou hast been Thou forever wilt be.*

*Pardon for sin and a peace that endureth,
Thine own dear presence to cheer and to guide,
Strength for today and bright hope for tomorrow,
Blessings all mine, with ten thousand beside!*

"Great Is Thy Faithfulness"
Thomans O. Chisholm

Father, thank You for the Bible. Thank You that You are the King, the Creator. But You're not a Creator that is far away and removed from us. You're a Creator who has come to us in the person of Your Son. You are the one who cares enough to give Him up freely for us all, in order that as we trust in Him and rest in Him we might find ourselves bowing down before You, declaring Your majesty, and living in the light of Your grace. May it be so. For Jesus' sake I ask it.

Amen

SESSION 05
God and Man

Additional Resources

Online Resources
Sermons, articles, and devotions can be found by scanning the QR code or by visiting tfl.org/christian-faith-list.

Sermons by Alistair

- "God's Basic Design"
- "Knowing God"

Articles & Devotions

- "Behold Your God: Creator, Counselor, Controller, and Comforter"
- "The Ultimate Reality"
- "A God-Given Burden"

Recommended Books

- *The Existence and Attributes of God* by Stephen Charnock
- *Created in God's Image* by Anthony A. Hoekema

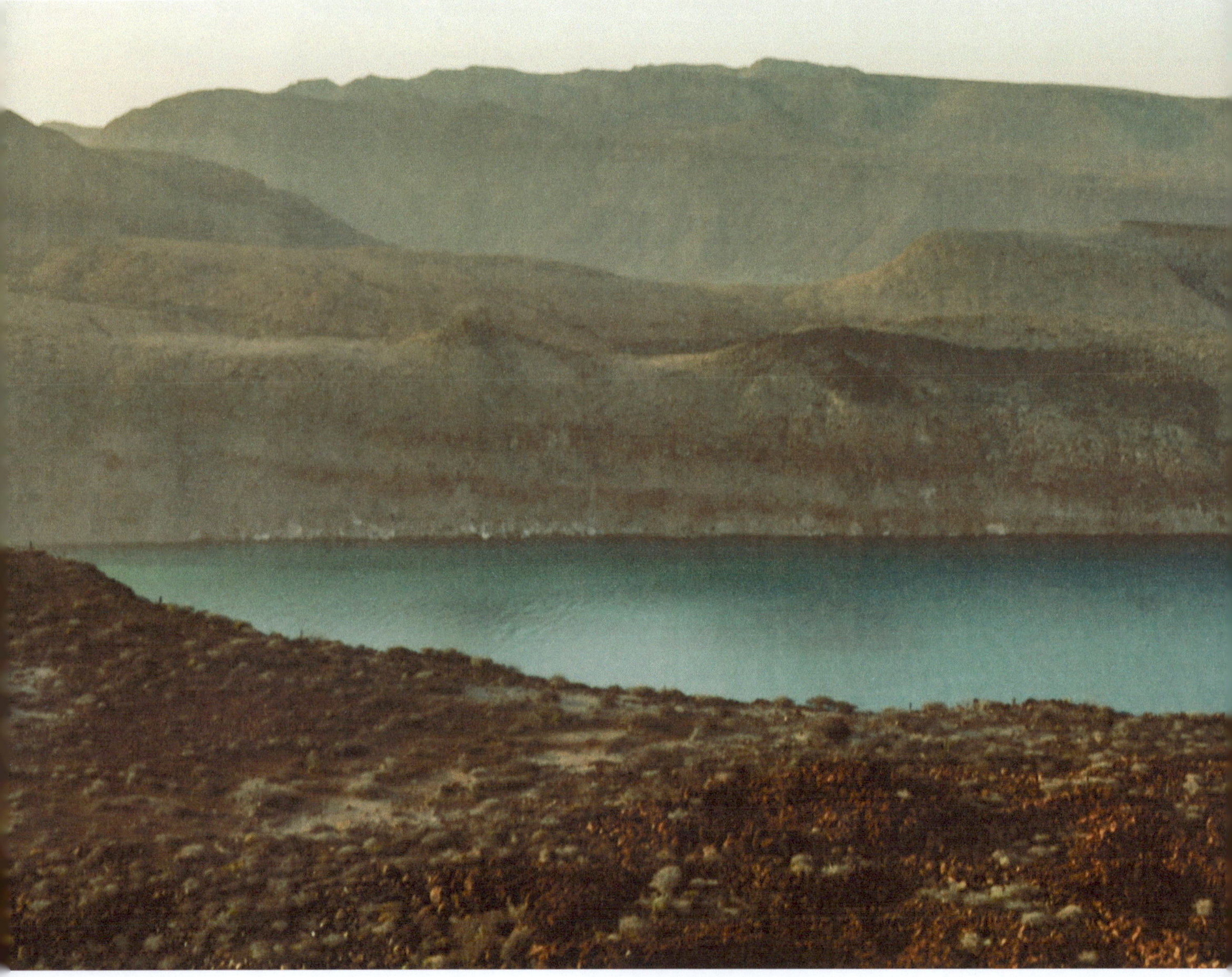

SESSION

06

The Authentic Jesus

> "
>
> It is only in light of the fact of Jesus' divinity
> that we can understand His humanity.
>
> ALISTAIR BEGG

01

Note to Leader: While it's difficult to comprehend how Jesus is fully human and fully God, Scripture is filled with support for both. Be prepared to point to relevant, helpful passages.

SESSION 06

The Authentic Jesus

Getting Started

01. What are the first five words that come to mind when you think about Jesus?

02. How might you explain who Jesus is to someone who has never heard of Him?

📖 **Read Matthew 16:13–20 and answer the questions below.**

01. What do these verses teach us about Jesus' identity?

02. How was Peter able to correctly answer Jesus' question?

02

Listen to "The Authentic Jesus"

Scan the QR code or visit tfl.org/christian-faith.

SESSION 06

The Authentic Jesus

Listen & Learn

Who is Jesus? Since His incarnation, people have confused and disparaged the identity of the Son of God. Alistair teaches who Jesus is according to the Bible, emphasizing His true nature as fully human and fully God. These two qualities exist without conflict or division and affirm His authority over life and death. In a world full of misguided notions about the identity of Jesus, it is only by looking to Scripture that we can understand the truth about Him.

A right understanding of Jesus' nature is not only necessary for our own salvation but also essential to our witness to others. The purpose of this lesson is to help you understand both the divine and human nature of Jesus.

Key Terms
docetism
a heresy, or false teaching, that denies Jesus' humanity, claiming that because He is fully divine, He only *seemed* human (from the Greek word *dokein*, meaning "to appear")
Arianism
a heresy that denies the deity of Jesus, instead claiming that He was created by God the Father

Fill in the Blank

01. "Jesus, while true _____, is also true _____."

02. "In Christ, _____ natures exist 'without _____, without _____, without _____,' and 'without _____.'"

Short Answer

01. What does Alistair say Jesus' birth was like, aside from His supernatural conception?

02. What happens when we try to lessen Jesus' humanity in an effort to emphasize His divinity?

Notes

Additional notes on page 68

03

SESSION 06

The Authentic Jesus

Going Deeper

01. In what ways is the true humanity of Jesus a comfort for the Christian? Why is it essential that we uphold this doctrine?

02. How would you respond to someone who says that Jesus is not God because the New Testament doesn't say that He is God?

03. Revisit your answer to question 2 in Getting Started. Is there anything you would change?

Notes Continued...

SESSION 06
The Authentic Jesus

Praise & Prayer

*Let earth and heaven combine,
Angels and men agree,
To praise, in songs divine,
The incarnate Deity,
Our God contracted to a span,
Incomprehensibly made man.*

"Let Earth and Heaven Combine"
Charles Wesley

My God and Father, thank You that You have not left us to ourselves to wander around in the wilderness of our collapsing communities but that you have come to seek us out, a Shepherd looking for lost sheep, a Savior coming to forgive and to cleanse, and a King coming to reign. Thank You for loving us so much. Thank You that the story of Your kingdom does not wind down to a sorry conclusion but rather that You reign forever, and in Christ You have invited us to reign with You.

Amen

SESSION 06

The Authentic Jesus

Additional Resources

Online Resources
Sermons, articles, and devotions can be found by scanning the QR code or by visiting tfl.org/christian-faith-list.

Sermons by Alistair

- *To Know Christ*
- *Who Is Jesus?*

Articles & Devotions

- "Jesus Christ: Humble Servant"
- "The Pre-Existent Word"
- "The Oldest Christian Confession"

Recommended Books

- *The Person and Work of Christ* by B. B. Warfield
- *Name above All Names* by Alistair Begg and Sinclair B. Ferguson
- *The Incomparable Christ* by John Stott

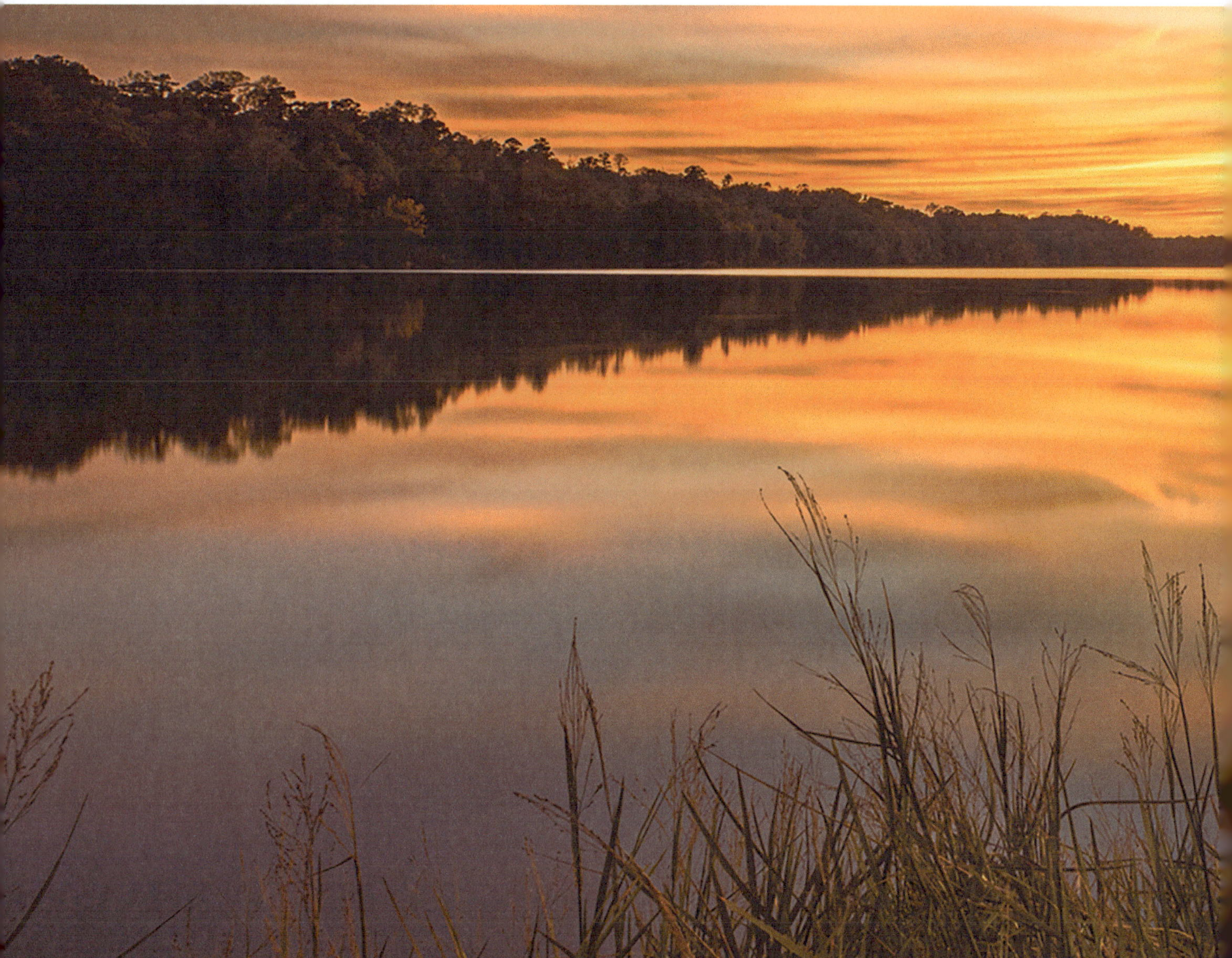

SESSION

07

The Holy Spirit

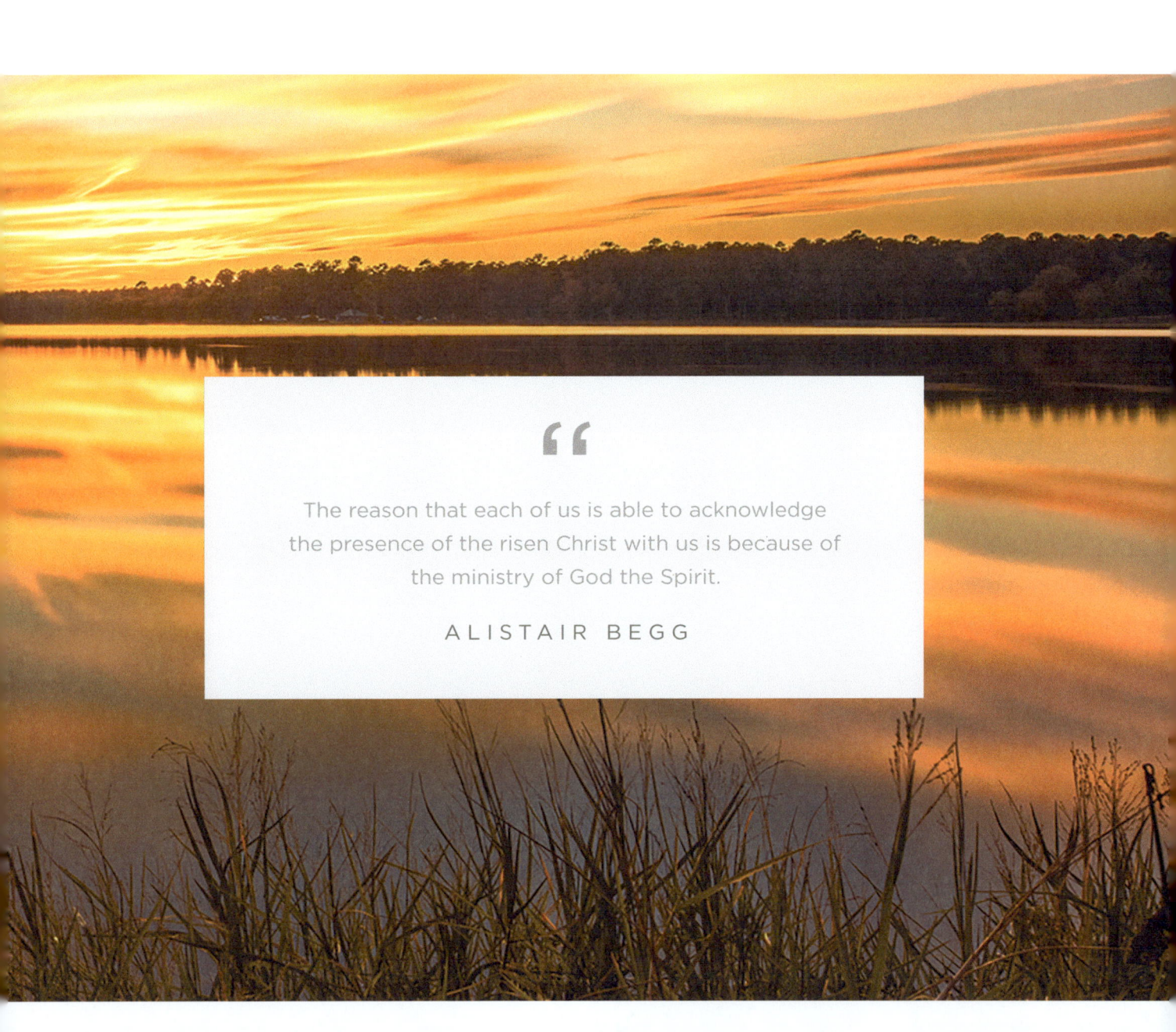

> "
>
> The reason that each of us is able to acknowledge the presence of the risen Christ with us is because of the ministry of God the Spirit.
>
> ALISTAIR BEGG

01

Note to Leader: Before you meet with your friend, write down and prepare to share ways that you have seen the Holy Spirit at work in your own life.

SESSION 07

The Holy Spirit

Getting Started

01. What are the first five words that come to mind when you think about the Holy Spirit?

02. What questions do you have about the Holy Spirit?

Read John 16:8–15 and answer the questions below.

01. According to Jesus, what would the Holy Spirit do to the world when He would come?

02. What did Jesus promise that the Holy Spirit would do for His followers?

02

Listen to "The Holy Spirit"
Scan the QR code or visit tfl.org/christian-faith.

SESSION 07
The Holy Spirit

Listen & Learn

As the time of His crucifixion drew near, Jesus explained to His disciples why He had to depart and promised to send a Helper: the Holy Spirit. Contrary to some misunderstandings, this Holy Spirit is no mere force; He is a person who has been active since creation. Walking us through the activity of the third person of the Trinity, Alistair explains that it is the work of God's Spirit poured out on God's people that conforms us to the image of His Son, Jesus Christ.

Unless you know the important role that the Holy Spirit plays in the Christian life, you will labor and strive to bear spiritual fruit in vain. The purpose of this lesson is to help you to understand the Holy Spirit's role in the life of the believer so that you will be able to glorify God through His powerful work in your life.

> **Key Terms**
>
> **pneumatology**
> the study of the Holy Spirit
>
> **modalism**
> a heresy claiming that there is one God who appears in three modes: sometimes as the Father, sometimes as the Son, and sometimes as the Spirit

Fill in the Blank

01. "It is impossible to explain the life of _____ apart from His _____ with the other members of the _____."

02. "What the Father _____ the Son comes to procure and to provide by way of _____; and what the Son provides by way of _____ the Holy Spirit then comes to _____ to the lives of those who believe."

Short Answer

01. What event recorded in the Bible fulfilled Jesus' promise in John 16? (See Acts 2.)

02. What is the Holy Spirit's role in creation?

Notes

Additional notes on page 78

SESSION 07

The Holy Spirit

Going Deeper

01. Many errors arise in the church and in Christian living because the Holy Spirit and His work are misunderstood. What truths about the Holy Spirit will help you to discern whether a "work of the Spirit" is authentic?

02. It is right for Christians to emphasize the importance of sound theology and the need to live by biblical principles—but these alone do not guarantee that Christ will be glorified. Why are these good things insufficient apart from the empowering presence of the Holy Spirit?

03. How can you become more dependent upon the Holy Spirit in your own life and service?

Notes Continued...

SESSION 07
The Holy Spirit

Praise & Prayer

Spirit of God, who dwells within my heart,
Wean it from sin, through all its pulses move.
Stoop to my weakness, mighty as You are,
And make me love You as I ought to love.

Teach me to love You as Your angels love,
One holy passion filling all my frame:
The fullness of the heaven-descended Dove;
My heart an altar, and Your love the flame.

"Spirit of God,
Descend upon My Heart"
George Croly

God, thank You that you have poured out Your Spirit in these last days. Thank You that in Christ all believers have been baptized into one Spirit. And yet I realize how easy it is to grieve the Spirit, to quench His work by my pride, by my disobedience, by my toleration of jealousy and animosity, by my unkind thoughts and bitter words.

In the same way as I often need to go to those whom I love most and say, "I never should have done that, and I am sorry," so I need to come to You, Holy Spirit, and say the same. Please pick me up in Your embrace. Fill me so that Christ may be increasingly precious to me and so that I may be increasingly conformed to His image.

Come and meet with me, Lord. Come and pour out Your Spirit and, as Habakkuk prayed, "revive Your work in the midst of the years."[1] I pray this in Jesus' name.

Amen

---
[1] Habakkuk 3:2 (NASB).

SESSION 07
The Holy Spirit

Additional Resources

Online Resources
Sermons, articles, and devotions can be found by scanning the QR code or by visiting tfl.org/christian-faith-list.

Sermons by Alistair

- "The Indwelling Spirit"
- "The Age of fthe Spirit"

Articles & Devotions

- "Who Is the Holy Spirit?"
- "The Spirit's Power"
- "We Need You"

Recommended Books

- *The Holy Spirit* by Sinclair B. Ferguson
- *Who on Earth Is the Holy Spirit?* by Tim Chester
- *Keep in Step with the Spirit* by J. I. Packer

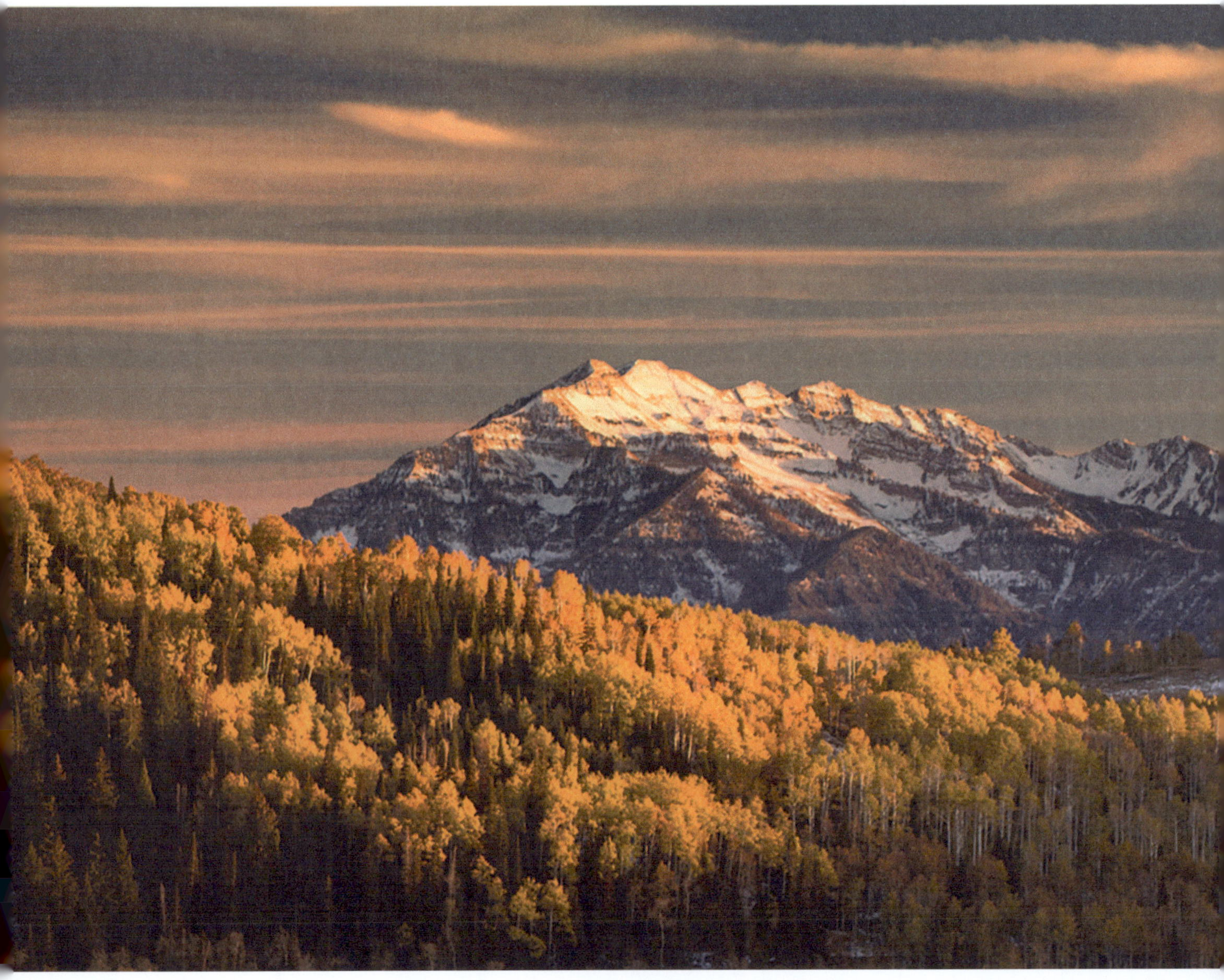

SESSION

08

"All Prayer"

> Do you realize what an amazing privilege that is, that you are able to go to the living God, the creator of the ends of the earth, and seek Him on behalf of a brother or a sister?
>
> ALISTAIR BEGG

01

Note to Leader: Consider asking your friend to open or close your meeting time in prayer if this is something you haven't done up to this point.

SESSION 08

"All Prayer"

Getting Started

01. How would you define prayer for someone who is not a Christian?

02. Are you satisfied with your prayer life? If not, in what ways would you like to see growth?

📖 **Read Ephesians 6:16–18 and answer the questions below.**

01.   What do you think it means to pray "in the Spirit"?

02.   Why do you think Paul encourages us to pray with all perseverance?

Listen to "All Prayer"

Scan the QR code or visit tfl.org/christian-faith.

02

SESSION 08

"All Prayer"

Listen & Learn

> **Key Terms**
>
> **ACTS**
>
> a common acrostic prayer model that encourages prayers of *adoration, confession, thanksgiving,* and *supplication*

Christians know that prayer is essential, but we often struggle with knowing how to pray best. As Paul instructed the Ephesians in wielding the spiritual weapon of prayer, he both exemplified and explained how to pray, when to pray, and what to pray for. Walking us through Paul's imperatives on prayer, Alistair helps us understand what it means to pray continually, varyingly, and perseveringly for all our brothers and sisters in Christ with God-centered perspective and trust.

Through prayer, we praise and thank God, confess our sins to Him, and express our dependence upon Him as we seek His help in matters both great and small. This session provides instruction regarding prayer so that you will know how to pray and be able to teach other Christians how to pray effectively.

Fill in the Blank

01. "This call to 'all prayer' is an expression of our _____ upon God. It's not _____; it is _____, because actually, it is impossible for us to enjoy an intimate relationship with God without it."

02. "Learning to pray _____ by the Holy Spirit and _____ by the Scriptures will inevitably focus our eyes on the _____ and the _____ of God and the _____ of the church."

PAGE 82 THE BASICS OF THE CHRISTIAN FAITH

Short Answer

01. What does it mean to pray with adoration?

02. What does it mean to pray with confession?

03. What does it mean to pray with thanksgiving?

04. What does it mean to pray with supplication?

Notes

Additional notes on page 88

03

SESSION 08

"All Prayer"

Going Deeper

01. Why is it important to avoid turning prayer into a list of requests for God? How might you guard against this going forward?

02.   What truths about God encourage you to persevere in prayer?

Notes Continued...

SESSION 08
"All Prayer"

Praise & Prayer

*Prayer is the soul's sincere desire,
Expressed in thought or word,
The burning of a hidden fire,
A longing for the Lord.*

*Prayer is the secret battleground
Where victories are won;
By prayer the will of God is found
And work for Him begun.*

**"Prayer Is the
Soul's Sincere Desire"**
James Montgomery

"*O*ur Father in heaven, hallowed be your name. Your kingdom come, your will be done, on earth as it is in heaven. Give us this day our daily bread, and forgive us our debts, as we also have forgiven our debtors. And lead us not into temptation, but deliver us from evil." (Matt. 6:9-13)

Amen

SESSION 08

"All Prayer"

Additional Resources

Online Resources
Sermons, articles, and devotions can be found by scanning the QR code or by visiting tfl.org/christian-faith-list.

Sermons by Alistair

- *A Study in Luke,* vol. 7: *When You Pray, Say...*
- "Asking God for Wisdom"

Articles & Devotions

- "How to Approach God in Prayer"
- "Praying at All Times"
- "God Hears Our Cries"

Recommended Books

- *Practical Prayer* by Derek Prime
- *Praying the Bible* by Donald S. Whitney
- *Pray Big* by Alistair Begg

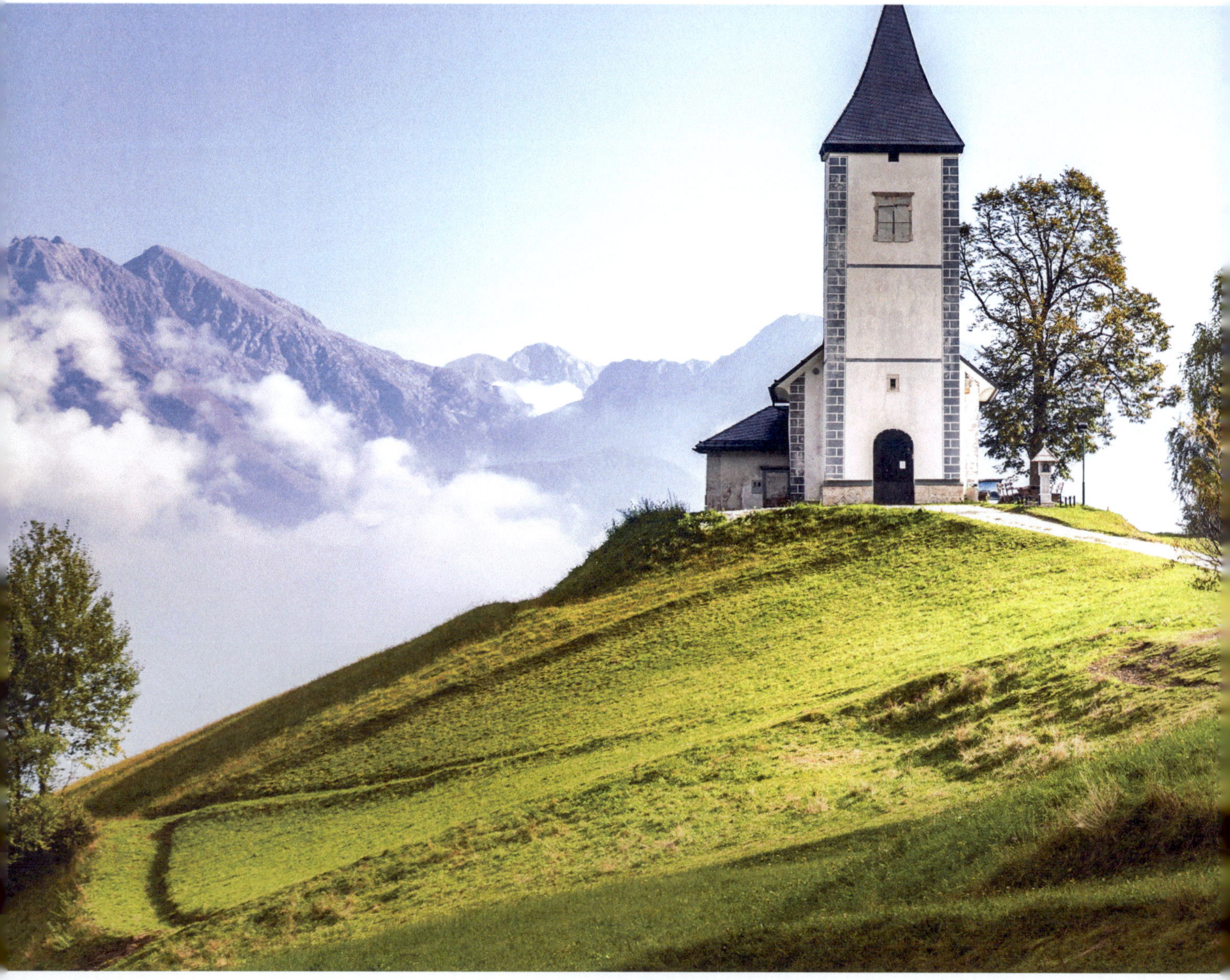

SESSION

09

Who or What Is the Church?

> "
>
> There would be no such thing as 'the church' were it not for the fact that God from all of eternity planned to have a people that are His very own.
>
> ALISTAIR BEGG

01

> **Note to Leader**
>
> Some of the questions in this session intentionally assume involvement with other believers in a local church body. If your friend is not involved, you may want to consult this session's additional resources to be better prepared for your meeting.

SESSION 09

Who or What Is the Church?

Getting Started

01. What are some things—either good or bad—that come to mind when you think about the church?

02. How are you involved in the church?

📖 **Read Ephesians 2:19–22 and answer the questions below.**

01. According to Paul, what is the foundation of the church?

02. What imagery does Paul use to describe the church? What does this teach you about the church?

02

Listen to "Who or What Is the Church?"
Scan the QR code or visit tfl.org/christian-faith.

SESSION 09

Who or What Is the Church?

Listen & Learn

Does the church have any relevance for the twenty-first century? By explaining the divine origins of the church, the truth about membership in the church, and how the Bible defines the church, Alistair helps us answer this question. Jesus Christ is the foundation of the church, and this one truth forms the cornerstone for all we believe about it.

God has entrusted the task of discipleship to the local church. Therefore, it is very important for every Christian to understand God's design for the local church and its place in the Christian life. The aim of this session is to help you grow in your understanding of the local church so that you will be increasingly devoted to it.

Key Terms

the local church
a local gathering of believers that meets regularly and follows the pattern set forth by the early church (see Acts 2:42-47)

the universal church
also sometimes called the catholic (with a small *c*) church; the body of all believers around the world

the visible church
the church as we see it (i.e., those who are part of an identifiable church entity as a result of external gatherings, religious interest, heritage, baptism, family tradition, etc.)

the invisible church
the church as God sees it (i.e., all believers, past, present, and future)

Fill in the Blank

01. "The church is not a _____ invention; it is a _____ institution."

02. "Membership in the church is not a matter of _____ attachment but of _____ union."

03. "The real church is clearly _____, comprising _____ of every age who have been included in _____, scattered throughout _____ of the world in _____ kinds of places."

Short Answer

01.   What does Alistair teach about the church's divine origin?

Notes

Additional notes on page 98

03

SESSION 09
Who or What Is the Church?

Going Deeper

01. If someone asks you how to become a part of the church, how should you answer?

02. While we are saved individually because of our personal union with the Lord Jesus Christ, the Christian life is never meant to be only a matter of personal experience. It also entails fellowship with other believers. Why is important to view the Christian life in terms of corporate commitment and not only in terms of private experience?

Notes Continued...

SESSION 09
Who or What Is the Church?

Praise & Prayer

*The church's one foundation
Is Jesus Christ, her Lord;
She is His new creation
By water and the Word.
From heav'n He came and sought her
To be His holy bride;
With His own blood He bought her,
And for her life He died.*

"The Church's One Foundation"
Samuel John Stone

God grant that I may be completely unsettled and unresting until I am assured that I am included in Christ, by grace and through faith. Give me love and zeal for Your bride, the church, for all my days. And grant that I will increasingly be convinced of my need for fellowship with Your people in the context of the church.

Amen

SESSION 09

Who or What Is the Church?

Additional Resources

Online Resources
Sermons, articles, and devotions can be found by scanning the QR code or by visiting tfl.org/christian-faith-list.

Sermons by Alistair

- *What Is the Church?*
- *Seven Marks of an Effective Church*

Articles & Devotions

- "Alistair Begg on Finding a Church"
- "Together Is Where We Belong"
- "A Gospel Church"

Recommended Books

- *Devoted to God's Church* by Sinclair B. Ferguson
- *Corporate Worship* by Matt Merker

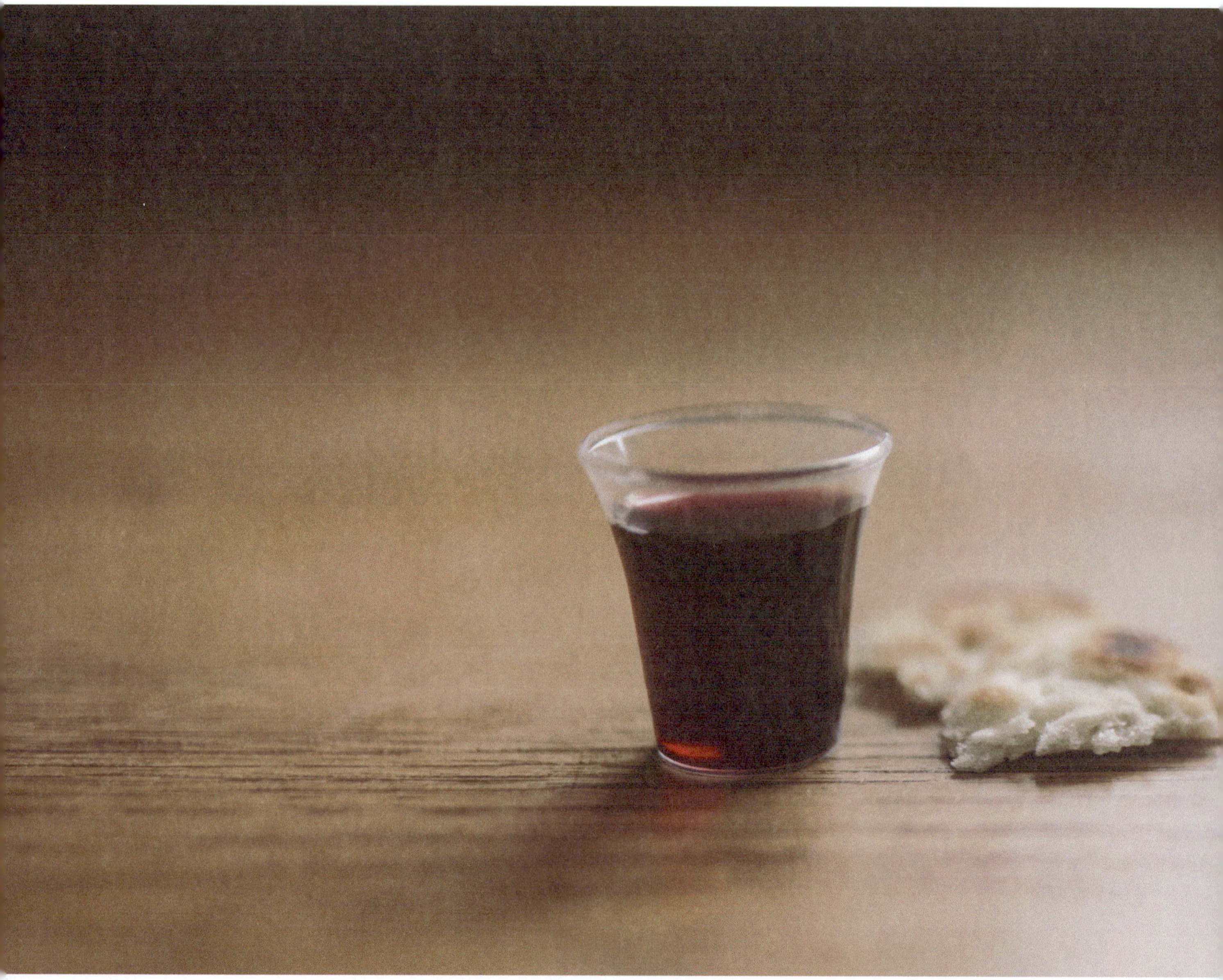

SESSION

10

The Sacraments

> "
> The sacraments—baptism and the Lord's Supper—do not signify, don't teach us, any other truths than the truths that are taught in the Bible.
>
> ALISTAIR BEGG

Note to Leader

As you will see, Alistair's teaching on baptism does not go into much depth in this message. He more clearly articulates his views on baptism in two of the sermons in this session's **Additional Resources**

SESSION 10

The Sacraments

Getting Started

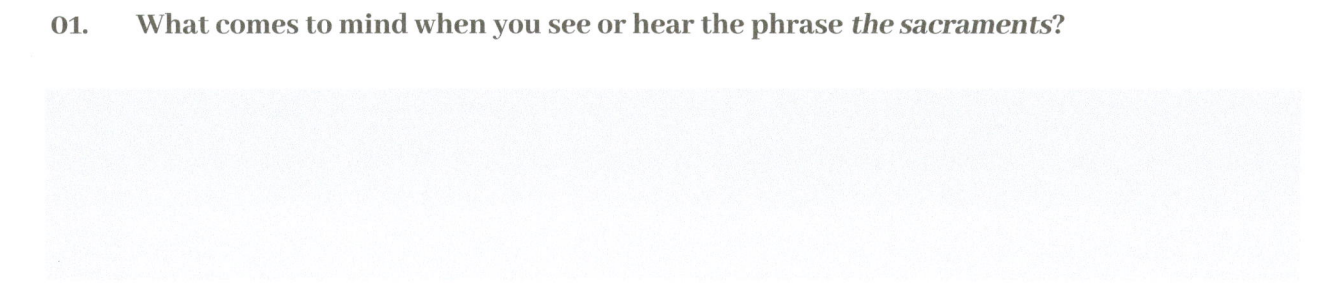

01. What comes to mind when you see or hear the phrase *the sacraments*?

02. What is your current understanding of the Lord's Supper and its significance?

02. Have you been baptized? If so, when and why? If not, why haven't you done so?

📖 **Read Acts 2:42–47 and answer the questions below.**

01. What was the local church in Acts 2 committed to?

02. What are some notable characteristics of that church?

Listen to "The Sacraments"
Scan the QR code or visit tfl.org/christian-faith.

SESSION 10
The Sacraments

Listen & Learn

Key Term

sacraments
outward and visible signs of an inward and spiritual grace that were ordained by God

The sacraments are outward, visible signs of inward, invisible grace—but we must not confuse the sign with the thing signified! Alistair helps us to distinguish between the symbols of baptism and the Lord's Supper and the realities to which they point. These ordinances are given to believers as commands from Christ in order to commemorate and proclaim Him. When we share in them, our faith is strengthened and our anticipation for Christ's return grows.

The sacraments have been given to the church so that He might be remembered and proclaimed in the church until He comes again. They must therefore never be downplayed or ignored. In this lesson, you will learn the important role that the sacraments play in your growth as a disciple of Jesus Christ.

Fill in the Blank

01. "The reality to which [the sacraments] point is _____, not _____."

02. List the five characteristics of the Lord's Supper:

  a. It is an _____ in which we _____ Christ.

  b. It is a _____ in which we _____ Christ.

  c. It is a _____ in which we _____ Christ.

  d. It is a _____ in which we _____ on Christ.

  e. It is an _____ in which we _____ for Christ.

Short Answer

01. According to Protestants, how many sacraments are there, and what are they?

02. What is the Roman Catholic view of the Lord's Supper?

Notes

Additional notes on page 108

03

SESSION 10

The Sacraments

Going Deeper

01. There are clear differences between the Roman Catholic view of the sacraments and the Protestant view. What are some of the key differences, and why do they matter?

02. The Lord's Supper is not just a religious ritual or a symbolic reminder of Christ's death. Rather, God spiritually meets with His people as they participate in the Lord's Supper. How does this understanding of the Lord's Supper elevate its importance?

03. While Alistair focuses most of his attention in this sermon on a survey of the sacraments and an explanation of the Lord's Supper, he teaches the following truths about baptism: it's a matter of obedience for believers, and it doesn't add to what is taught in the Bible. According to Scripture, what do we know about baptism? (Consider reading passages such as Acts 2:37–38; 8:26–38; Rom. 6:3–4; Eph. 4:4–6; and Col. 2:8–14.)

Notes Continued...

SESSION 10

The Sacraments

Praise & Prayer

*Guide me, O my great Redeemer,
Pilgrim through this barren land;
I am weak, but You are mighty;
Hold me with Your powerful hand.
Bread of heaven, bread of heaven,
Feed me now and evermore.*

**"Guide Me,
O Thou Great Jehovah"**
William Williams

O God my Father, how I long for the clarity of Your truth to dawn upon my mind, for the immensity of Your love to grip my heart afresh, and for the wonder of Your dealings to frame my activities. I pray that You would save me from seeing Your sacraments as mere routine. Instead, when I partake in the Lord's Supper or witness baptisms, help me to look back in wonder, to look around in gratitude, and to look forward in anticipation. Amaze me again and again with Your abounding grace.

Amen

SESSION 10

The Sacraments

Additional Resources

Online Resources
Sermons, articles, and devotions can be found by scanning the QR code or by visiting tfl.org/christian-faith-list.

Sermons by Alistair

- "The Biblical Basis for Baptism"
- "The Nature and Meaning of the Lord's Supper"
- "The Baptism Debate"

Articles & Devotions

- "6 Bible Verses on Baptism"
- "Saved by Sacrifice"

Recommended Books

- *Baptism: Three Views* by Sinclair B. Ferguson, Anthony N. S. Lane, and Bruce A. Ware
- *Truth We Can Touch* by Tim Chester
- *The Lord's Supper: Remembering and Proclaiming Christ until He Comes*, edited by Thomas R. Schreiner and Matthew R. Crawford

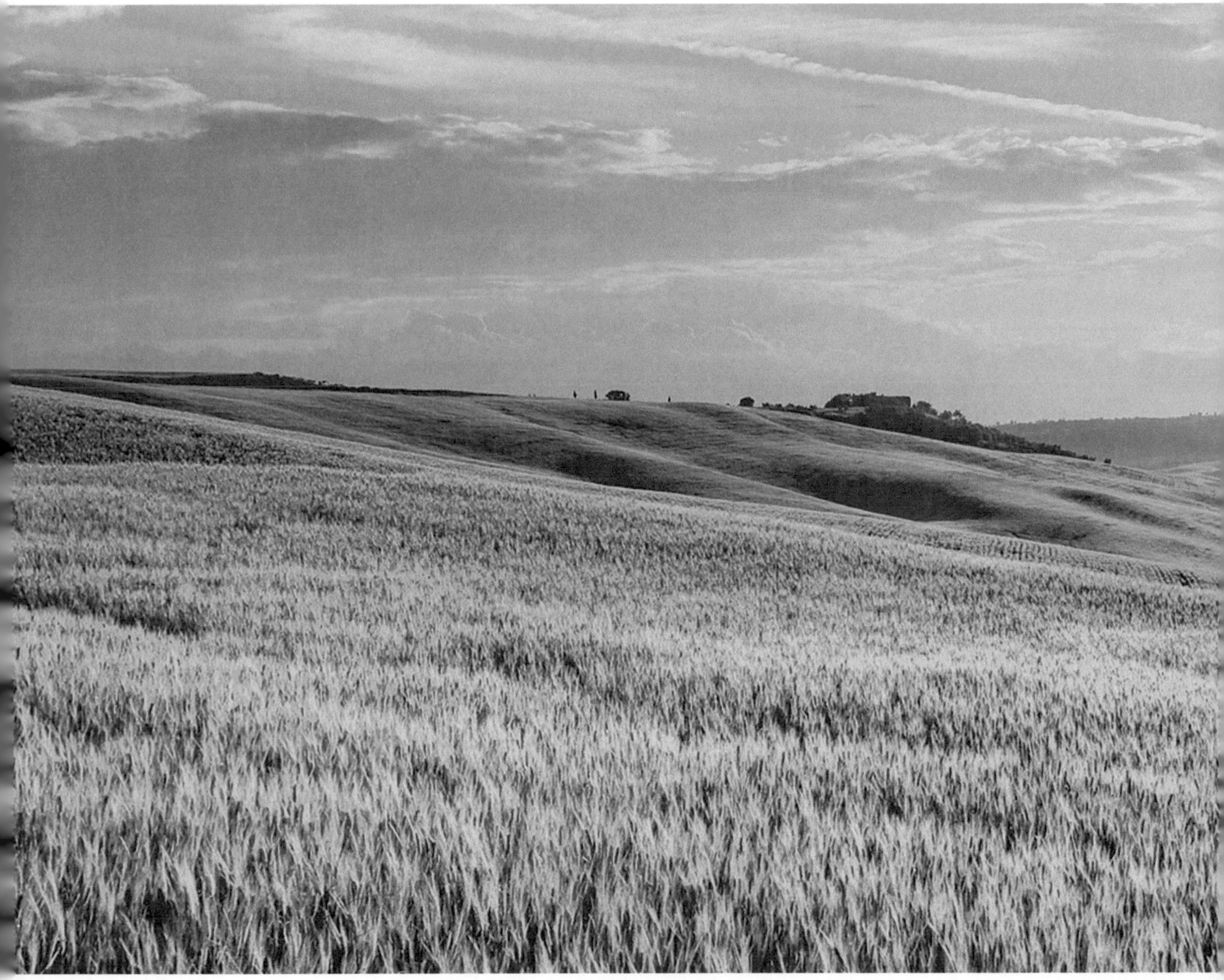

SESSION

11

Keeping His Commands

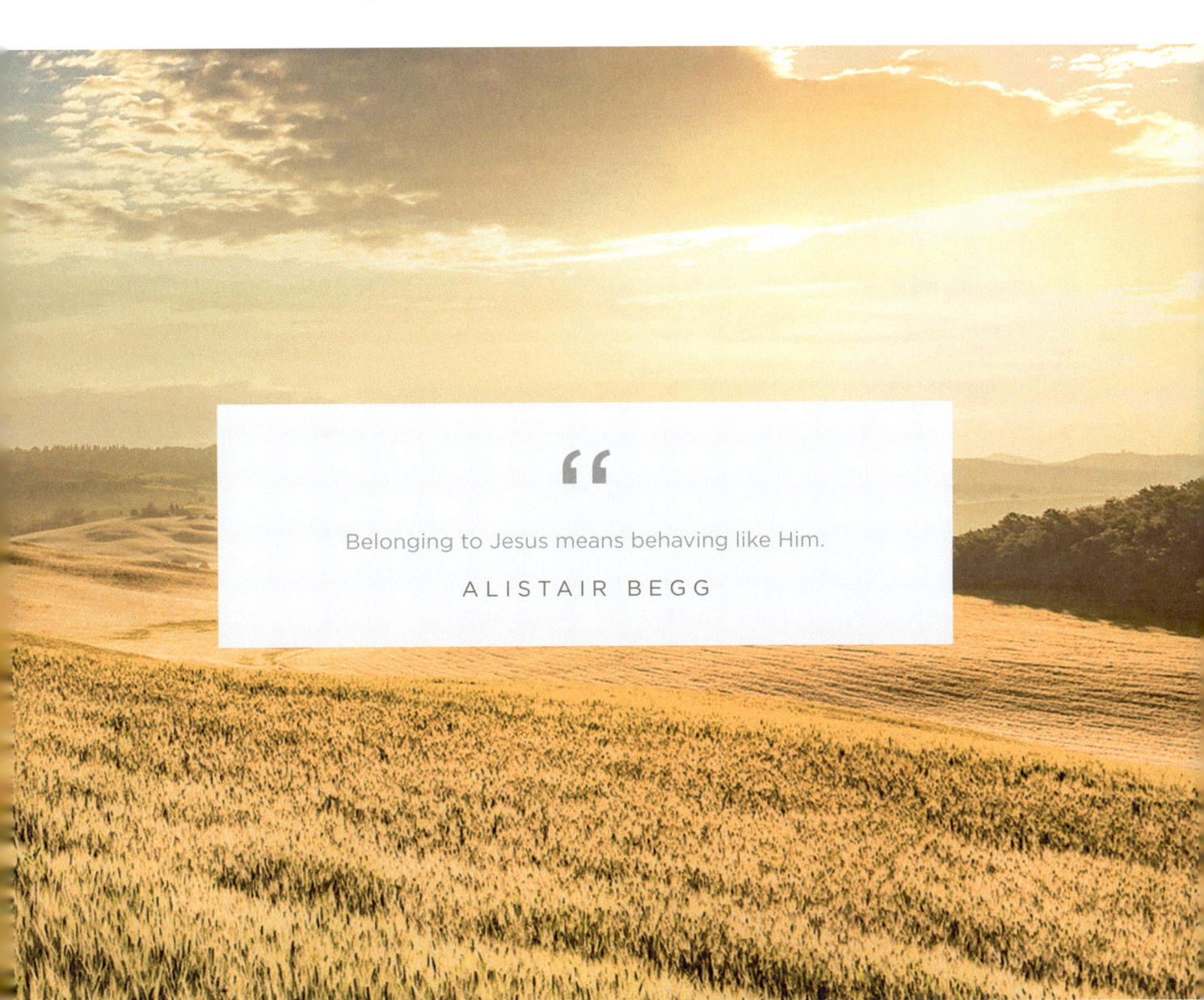

> "
>
> Belonging to Jesus means behaving like Him.
>
> ALISTAIR BEGG

01

Note to Leader: Nearly every believer has a natural inclination toward either legalism or antinomianism. As you complete this session, consider your disposition and how you guard against it. Help your friend work through that as well.

SESSION 11

Keeping His Commands

Getting Started

01. What does it mean to behave like Jesus?

02. When you hear the word *obedience*, what comes to mind?

📖 **Read 1 John 2:3–11 and answer the questions below.**

01. What are the marks of someone who knows God?

02. What is the "new commandment"? What does disobeying it reveal?

02

Listen to "Keeping His Commands"
Scan the QR code or visit tfl.org/christian-faith.

SESSION 11

Keeping His Commands

Listen & Learn

The apostle John issued a clear warning to the early church against those who professed Christ yet maintained sinful, self-centered lifestyles. Alistair explains that in contrast, genuine faith is marked by love for God's commandments and love for others. As Christians, our obedience should not feel like drudgery. Instead, our moral character should reflect our joyful belonging to Christ.

Obedience is an essential, yet often misunderstood, element of the Christian life. This session will help you consider how to joyfully obey Jesus in a manner that magnifies His finished work upon the cross.

Key Terms

antinomianism

from the Greek *anti* (against) and *nomos* (law); an unbiblical belief that there are no moral laws from God that believers are expected to obey

legalism

an unbiblical belief or way of living that emphasizes obedience to God's moral laws as the grounds for salvation and spiritual growth

Fill in the Blank

01. "Verbal _____ minus moral _____ is _____."

02. "Love _____ straight. Love _____ clearly. Love us from _____ into unbalanced judgments and conduct."

Short Answer

01. Which two "tests" from 1 John does Alistair unpack in this message?

02. While the ground of our salvation is in the atoning work of Jesus, what provides evidence of our salvation?

Notes

Additional notes on page 118

03

SESSION 11

Keeping His Commands

Going Deeper

01. Why is it appropriate and necessary to affirm that those who truly know God, although they still sin, are marked by their obedience to God's Word?

02.   In what ways is Christian love distinct from the world's understandings of love?

Notes Continued...

SESSION 11
Keeping His Commands

Praise & Prayer

When we walk with the Lord
In the light of His Word,
What a glory He sheds on our way!
While we do His good will,
He abides with us still,
And with all who will trust and obey.

Trust and obey, for there's no other way
To be happy in Jesus but to trust and obey.

"Trust and Obey"
John Henry Sammis

Father, write Your Word on my heart. Bring me, Lord, from a broad road that leads to destruction onto the narrow road that leads to life. Move me by Your grace from Dead End Street into the realm where life in all of its fullness is found in Christ. And then help me, by the power of the Holy Spirit, to increasingly be conformed to the image of Jesus, who did not come to be served but to serve and gave His life as a ransom for many. In His name I pray.

Amen

SESSION 11

Keeping His Commands

Additional Resources

Online Resources
Sermons, articles, and devotions can be found by scanning the QR code or by visiting tfl.org/christian-faith-list.

Sermons by Alistair

- *Pathway to Freedom*
- "Wholehearted Obedience"

Articles & Devotions

- "The Power and Mystery of Obedience"
- "The Paradox of Freedom in Christ"
- "What Does Obedience Have to Do with Following Jesus?"

Recommended Books

- *Devoted to God* by Sinclair B. Ferguson
- *The Mortification of Sin* by John Owen
- *Pathway to Freedom* by Alistair Begg

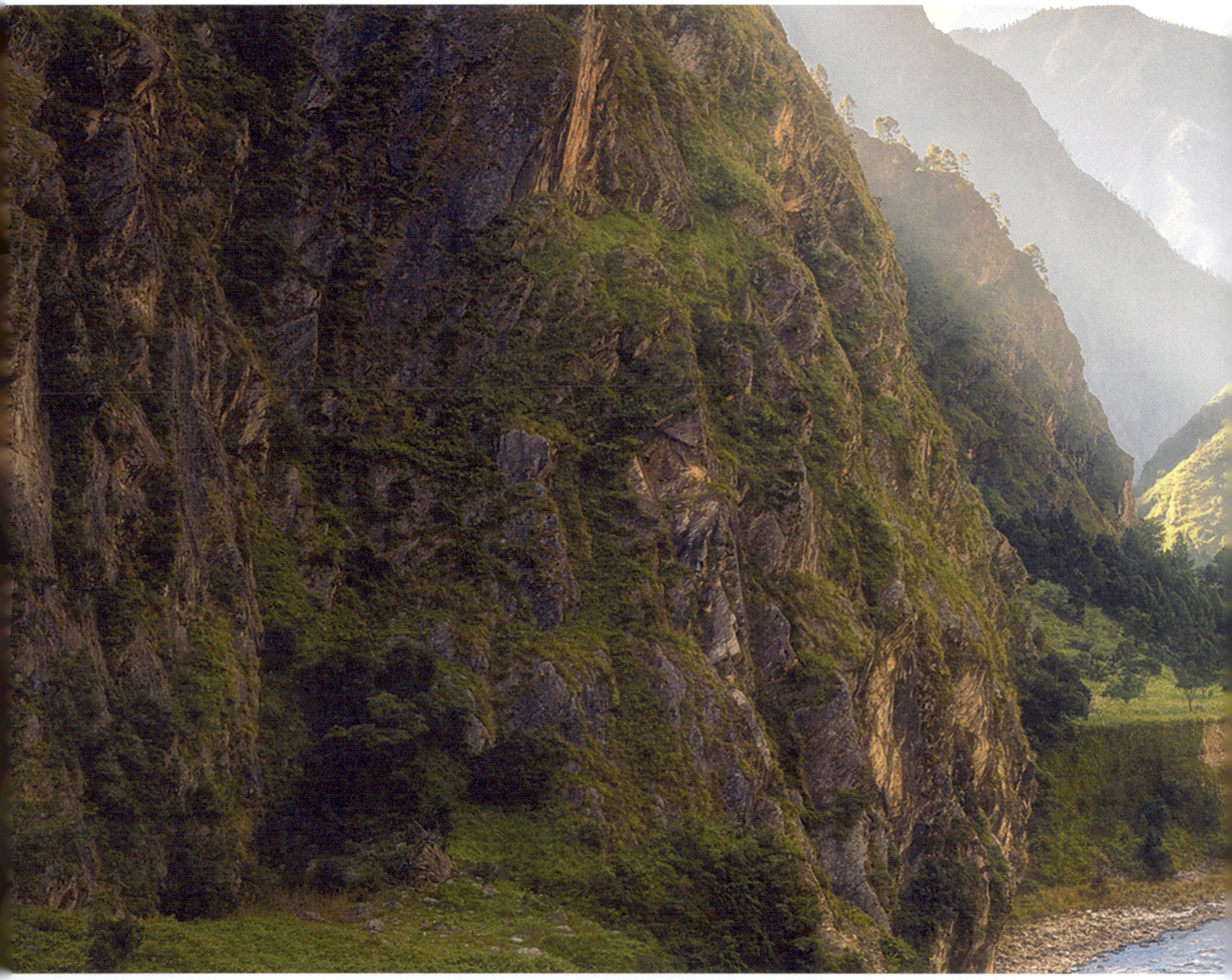

SESSION

12

Vital Signs

> "
> God is glorified as a result of the exercise of our spiritual gifts in the awareness of our divine enabling for the purpose of bringing glory to His name.
>
> ALISTAIR BEGG

01

Note to Leader: Be careful to avoid getting lost in tangential discussions about spiritual gifts. Focus on what Scripture says about their purpose.

SESSION 12

Vital Signs

Getting Started

01.   What are some traits that come to mind when you think about a healthy church?

02.   What are at least three specific ways that you can glorify God?

Read 1 Peter 4:7–11 and answer the questions below.

01. What are some of the spiritual gifts that are seen in the body of Christ?

02. Why should Christians always depend upon "the strength that God supplies" when using spiritual gifts?

Listen to "Vital Signs"

Scan the QR code or visit tfl.org/christian-faith.

02

SESSION 12
Vital Signs

Listen & Learn

> **Key Term**
>
> **spiritual gift**
>
> any ability that is given and enabled by God Himself and used in church ministry

In the same way that there are vital signs which show that the body is alive, there are vital signs that measure the health of Christ's body—the church. Alistair shares how prayer, love, hospitality, service, and worship are all necessary qualities for a church to have if it hopes to survive.

This session focuses on how the call to love and serve those around us is intertwined with the ultimate goal of giving glory to God.

Fill in the Blank

01. "Hospitality is simply _____ our doors and _____ people to _____ our _____ the way they are."

02. "There is nobody in the body of Christ who has not been _____ _____ under God."

Short Answer

01. According to Alistair's sermon, what are the five vital signs for any church?

PAGE 122 — THE BASICS OF THE CHRISTIAN FAITH

02. What are the two principles that undergird Christian service?

03. At one point in the sermon, Alistair asks, "How are we to serve in the body of Christ?" How does he then answer this question?

Notes

03

SESSION 12
Vital Signs

Going Deeper

01. In this sermon, Alistair quotes a hymn that says, "There's a work for Jesus none but you can do." Based on your current understanding of Scripture and feedback you have received from other believers, how has God gifted you to serve the church?

02. Why is dependence upon God's power essential for any ministry that aims to glorify Him alone?

03. What will it practically look like for you to minister in the strength that God supplies?

Notes Continued...

SESSION 12
Vital Signs

Praise & Prayer

I look not back; God knows the fruitless efforts,
The wasted hours, the sin, the deep regrets.
I leave them all with Him who blots the record,
And graciously forgives, and then forgets.

But I look up into the face of Jesus,
For there my heart can rest, my fears are stilled;
And there is joy, and love, and light for darkness,
And perfect peace, and ev'ry hope fulfilled.

"I Look Not Back"
Annie Johnson Flint

*T*hank You, Father, that Your purpose for Your people is to make us complete in Christ. I confess that as I consider vital signs of the believer, I often cringe in the awareness of my own weaknesses. But I want to thank You that the Son has said, "My grace is sufficient for you, for My power is made perfect in weakness."

It is Your blood and Your righteousness, Lord Jesus, that allows me to come boldly before Your throne of grace. I stand complete in You, knowing that I'm not what I once was, I'm not all I'm going to be, but I am different, by Your grace. And so I pray that I might heed Your commands and Your warnings, that You will pour out Your Spirit upon me in fresh measure, and that You will help me and guard me day by day. In Christ's name.

Amen

SESSION 12
Vital Signs

Additional Resources

Online Resources
Sermons, articles, and devotions can be found by scanning the QR code or by visiting tfl.org/christian-faith-list.

Sermons by Alistair

- *The Fruit of the Spirit*
- "The Priority of Prayer"
- "The Danger of Spiritual Paralysis"

Articles & Devotions

- "The New You"
- "Known by Their Fruit"
- "Four Ways You Can Please the Lord"

Recommended Books

- *The Fruitful Life* by Jerry Bridges
- *Living for God's Pleasure* by Derek Prime
- *Made for His Pleasure* by Alistair Begg

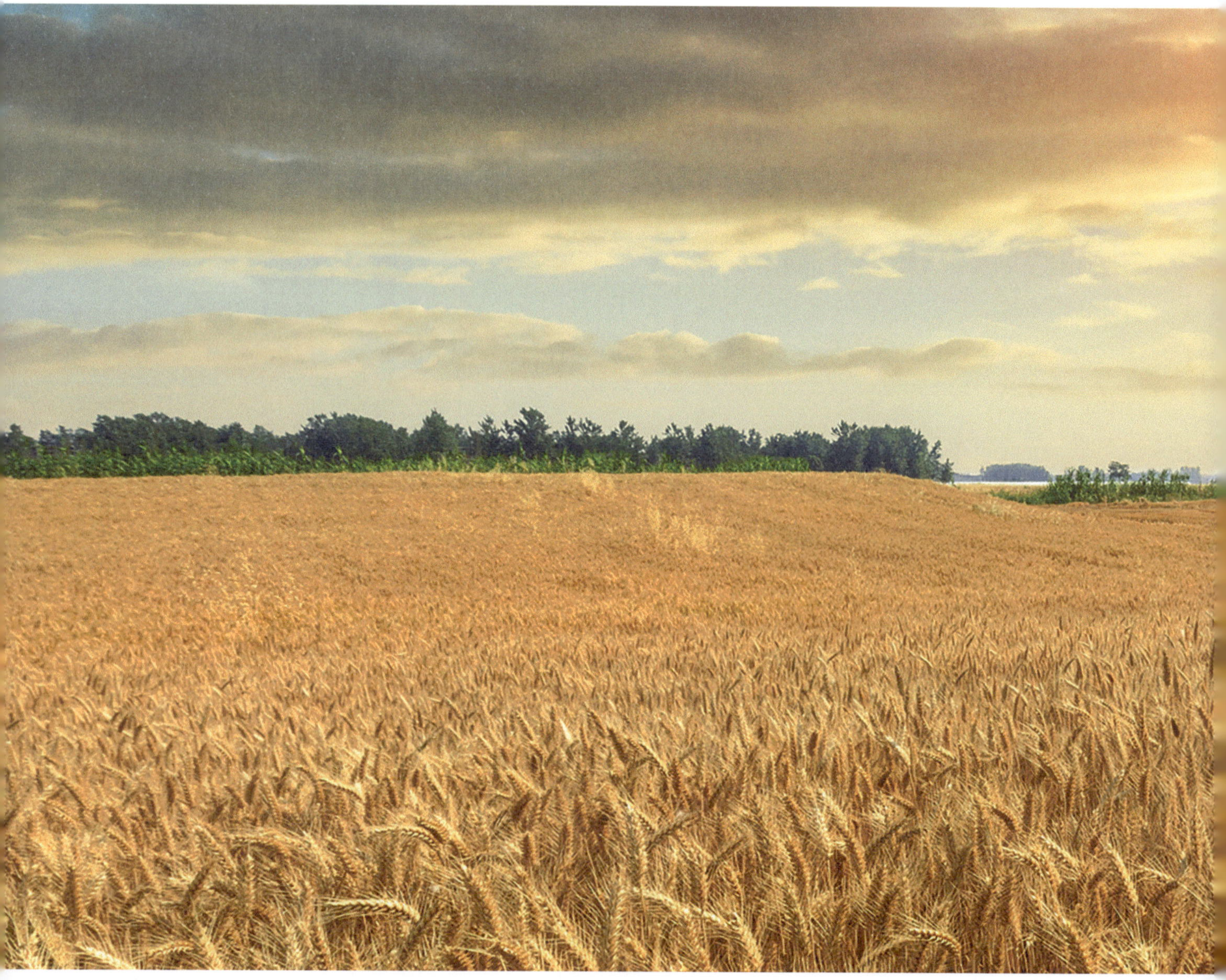

SESSION

13

Personal Evangelist

> "
>
> To every Christian that may be preoccupied with that which is helpful but not best, this exhortation rings out from the lips of Jesus: 'I tell you, lift up your eyes and look on the fields; they're white for harvest.'
>
> ALISTAIR BEGG

01

> **Note to Leader:** Evangelism is challenging for every believer but perhaps especially for new believers. It might be helpful for you to share examples of both successful and failed attempts at evangelism.

SESSION 13

Personal Evangelist

Getting Started

01. Is there anyone in your life whom you consider to be gifted at sharing the Gospel with others? If so, what about their approach stands out to you?

02. Is evangelism a normal part of your life? If so, explain how you approach it. If not, list a few reasons for why you don't routinely share your faith.

📖 **Read John 4:27–42 and answer the questions below.**

01. How is the Samaritan woman a good example of an evangelist?

02. What is the purpose of Jesus' teaching about sowing, reaping, and the harvest in verses 31–38? What are your main observations from this section?

Listen to "Personal Evangelist"
Scan the QR code or visit tfl.org/christian-faith.

02

SESSION 13

Personal Evangelist

Listen & Learn

> **Key Term**
>
> **evangelism**
>
> presenting Christ Jesus to sinful people in order that, through the power of the Holy Spirit, they may come to put their trust in God through Him[1]

When Jesus encountered the Samaritan woman at the well, His love and compassion for her provided a perfect model of evangelism. He began their conversation with a simple question—"Will you give me a drink?"—and ended it with a life-changing revelation: He was (and is) the Messiah. Alistair challenges us to emulate Jesus' approach to sharing our faith. As he reminds us, once we have had an encounter with Christ, we cannot help but become evangelists ourselves.

As important as it is for us to learn, grow, and be engaged with the church body, this session teaches that Christ has also called His followers to make disciples of all nations. This means that we must not become inwardly focused but should aim to reach those who do not yet know Jesus as Lord and Savior.

Fill in the Blank

01. "It is not evangelism—it is not the Gospel—to tell people that there are _____ that attach if they will _____ the Gospel. It is not the Gospel to tell people that there are great _____ that await them if they _____ the Gospel."

02. "The _____ is to tell people who _____ ____, why ____ _____, what ____ ____, why it _____, and that He is the self-proclaimed _____ of the world."

03. "Jesus is the only _____ because Jesus is the only one _____ to save."

---
[1] J. I. Packer, *Evangelism and the Sovereignty of God* (Downers Grove, IL: InterVarsity, 1961), 37–38, 40.

Short Answer

02. As it relates to evangelism, what does Alistair suggest happens when "we lose sight of the grandeur of the Gospel" and "take our eyes off Christ"?

03. How do unconverted people—the spiritually blind—realize they are blind?

Notes

Additional notes on page 138

SESSION 13

Personal Evangelist

Going Deeper

01. There are many places in Scripture where it seems that Jesus purposefully went out of His way for encounters with individuals. Why might this have been? In what ways can this motivate you to have evangelistic conversations?

02. How does Jesus' example encourage us to avoid being either too bombastic or too passive in our approach?

03. Have you had the opportunity to share the Gospel with people in the past? If so, what has (or has not) worked? And if not, what has held you back?

Notes Continued...

SESSION 13
Personal Evangelist

Praise & Prayer

*We've a story to tell to the nations
That shall turn their hearts to the right,
A story of truth and mercy,
A story of peace and light.*

*We've a Savior to show to the nations,
Who the path of sorrow has trod,
That all of the world's great peoples
Might come to the truth of God!*

"We've a Story to Tell to the Nations"
Henry Ernest Nichol

Write down the name of at least one unbeliever you know who needs to hear the Gospel, and write down a prayer for him or her. Pray that God will grant you love, boldness, and opportunities to share your faith.

SESSION 13

Personal Evangelist

Additional Resources

Online Resources
Sermons, articles, and devotions can be found by scanning the QR code or by visiting tfl.org/christian-faith-list.

Sermons by Alistair

- *Crossing the Barriers: A 12-Lesson Study on Evangelism*
- *FRANgelism: How to Witness to Friends, Relatives, Associates, and Neighbors*

Articles & Devotions

- "Gospel ABC"
- "Evangelism: God's Part and Ours"
- "A Matter of Concern"
- "The Gospel in a Godless City"

Recommended Books

- *Evangelism and the Sovereignty of God* by J. I. Packer
- *Honest Evangelism* by Rico Tice
- *Before You Share Your Faith* by Matt Smethurst

Answer Key

Note: Quotation marks around the answer indicate that it is a direct quote from Alistair's message. All other answers are summaries of Alistair's teaching.

Session 01

Fill in the Blank

01. "Salvation is not <u>by</u> works, but it is <u>for</u> works."

02. "There is only one way to be saved, and that is by doing two things: by turning from <u>my sin</u> and turning to <u>Christ</u>."

03. "There are two places that sin is punished: sin is punished in <u>hell</u>, and sin is punished at <u>Calvary</u>. And the message of the Gospel is '<u>Believe</u> in Jesus Christ today as your <u>Lord</u> and <u>Savior</u>, or face Him then as your rightful <u>Judge</u>.'"

Short Answer

01. "The word in Greek is *metanoéō*, which simply means 'to do an about turn.'" (According to the Westminster Shorter Catechism, Q. 87, "Repentance unto life is a saving grace, whereby a sinner, out of a true sense of his sin, and apprehension of the mercy of God in Christ, does, with grief and hatred of his sin, turn from it unto God, with full purpose of, and endeavor after, new obedience.")

02. "No. If that'd been the case, then Jesus Christ never need to have died upon the cross." Reread Ephesians 2:8–10.

Session 02

Fill in the Blank

01. "Jesus makes it clear by the time He steps on the stage of history, referencing the historicity of Adam and Eve, that the death that entered into the world was the <u>spiritual</u> death, closing down the <u>communion</u> between a holy God and His creation, bringing <u>alienation</u> into that picture, bringing bondage into people's lives, bringing conflict into their circumstances."

02. "Every one of us is <u>born</u> with an inherent <u>bias</u> to sin, every one of us a <u>sinner</u> in the same sinking ship with everybody else. And every day we are confronted by the ravaging nature of our condition."

03. "Sin is not an <u>intellectual</u> problem; it is a <u>moral</u> problem."

Short Answer

01. "Not only in the New Testament but also in the Old, we discover that leprosy is one of the clearest pictures ... that the Bible contains of the predicament of men and women as sinners. Like the leper, our lives are spoiled. We suffer not from this physical ailment, but we suffer by our natures from the leprosy of sin, the leprosy that has spoiled our souls."

02. "To become a Christian, trusting in what Jesus has done on the cross as our only basis for acceptance with God, will involve at least these three elements: One, acknowledging that I am absolutely helpless and cannot rely on any righteousness of my own ... secondly, believing that Jesus has died and has provided the very gift of righteousness that I've just admitted that I need; and thirdly, that on the strength of that I must then cast myself upon His mercy."

Session 03

Fill in the Blank

01. "It is impossible to go through the Letters without finding that again and again the apostles are urging upon their readers the absolute necessity of knowing <u>what</u> and <u>why</u> they believe."

02. "<u>Intellect</u> is not the key in learning Christian doctrine. <u>Obedience</u> is the key in learning Christian doctrine."

Short Answer

01. "The Spirit of God confirms for us the veracity of the Bible."

02. (1) the Trinity; (2) God's sovereignty; (3) Scripture's divine inspiration, infallibility, authority, and sufficiency; (4) humanity's universal sinfulness and guilt since the fall; (5) Christ's substitutionary atonement; (6) Christ's literal, physical resurrection from the dead; (7) the Holy Spirit's work in granting the believer repentance and faith; (8) the one holy, universal church to which all true believers belong; (9) the expectation of Christ's personal return in power and glory

Session 04

Fill in the Blank

01. "There is a part which in the table of contents is called the <u>Old Testament</u>, which goes from Genesis to Malachi, and then there is the <u>New Testament</u>, which goes from Matthew through to Revelation."

02. The Bible is "<u>sixty-six</u> books written in a variety of languages, mainly in <u>Hebrew</u> and <u>Greek</u>, over a period of more than a thousand years, originating in places as far apart as Babylon and Rome, and penned by as many as <u>forty</u> different individuals."

03. In the Old Testament, Jesus is <u>predicted</u>; in the Gospels, He is <u>revealed</u>; in the Acts of the Apostles, He is <u>preached</u>; in the Epistles, He is <u>explained</u>; and in the book of Revelation, He is <u>expected</u>.

Short Answer

01. "It is to make men and women wise unto salvation."

02. Scripture needs to be interpreted on the basis of the straightforward sense of the passage. Scripture needs to be interpreted by Scripture. The Bible can only be interpreted for us by the Holy Spirit, because true understanding is not natural to us. Scripture needs to be interpreted dynamically, being considered in its own time and context, placed in the framework of the whole purpose of Scripture, and then applied to our own lives.

Session 05

Fill in the Blank

01. "If we ask the question 'Who, then, is this God?' the first answer is that He is <u>Lord</u>."

02. "The story of Christianity is that the <u>creator</u> of the universe has stepped down into time. And indeed, He has done so because He <u>cares</u>."

Short Answer

01. "We have been made in the image of God ... He has made us in such a way that we might know Him; He has made us for a relationship with Himself."

02. "Man is both marked by a dignity as made in God's image, and he is also dealing with depravity as being a sinner before God's sight."

03. "We are unfit for His presence, we are actually insensitive to His Word, we're unrighteous before His law, and what we like to do is set our own rules, create our own examination papers, and then grade them ourselves."

04. "We will, in Christ, be awakened to a new day, to a new heaven and to a new earth, in which dwells righteousness."

Session 06

Fill in the Blank

01. "Jesus, while true <u>man</u>, is also true <u>God</u>."

02. "In Christ, <u>two</u> natures exist 'without <u>confusion</u>, without <u>change</u>, without <u>division</u>' and 'without <u>separation</u>.'"

Short Answer

01. It was remarkably normal.

02. "Any attempt to show that Jesus is God by diminishing His humanity is to introduce us to an unauthentic Jesus."

Session 07

Fill in the Blank

01. "It is impossible to explain the life of <u>Christ</u> apart from His <u>communion</u> with the other members of the <u>Trinity</u>."

02. "What the Father <u>plans</u> the Son comes to procure and to provide by way of <u>salvation</u>; and what the Son provides by way of <u>salvation</u> the Holy Spirit then comes to <u>apply</u> to the lives of those who believe."

Short Answer

01. "The giving of the Spirit—the pouring out of the Spirit in the unique and unrepeatable event of Pentecost—is the very promise that is alluded to here in John 16."

02. "The Holy Spirit was the agent of creation," and He "is the agent of God's new creation."

Session 08

Fill in the Blank

01. "This call to 'all prayer' is an expression of our <u>dependence</u> upon God. It's not <u>optional</u>; it is <u>essential</u>, because actually, it is impossible for us to enjoy an intimate relationship with God without it."

02. "Learning to pray <u>enabled</u> by the Holy Spirit and <u>guided</u> by the Scriptures will inevitably focus our eyes on the <u>Gospel</u> and the <u>glory</u> of God and the <u>purpose</u> of the church."

Short Answer

01. Adoration is approaching God in prayer by praising Him for who He is.

02. Confession is admitting to God the ways that we have sinned against Him.

03. Thanksgiving is expressing gratitude to God for what He has done, remembering the grace and mercy that He has shown to us regardless of our present circumstances.

04. Supplication is a petition or expression of needs, bringing our requests—for others and ourselves—to God.

Session 09

Fill in the Blank

01. "The church is not a <u>human</u> invention; it is a <u>divine</u> institution."

02. "Membership in the church is not a matter of <u>external</u> attachment but of <u>spiritual</u> union."

03. "The real church is clearly <u>invisible</u>, comprising <u>all</u> of every age who have been included in <u>Christ</u>, scattered throughout <u>all</u> of the world in <u>all</u> kinds of places."

Short Answer

01. "The Bible says that the church owes its origin not to man but to God. There is no such thing as 'the church' were it not for the fact that God from all of eternity planned to have a people that are His very own. And the solidarity and the corporate distinctiveness of the people of God, as distinct from all other communities, can be tied to only one thing—namely, to the call of God."

Session 10

Fill in the Blank

01. "The reality to which [the sacraments] point is <u>displayed</u>, not <u>dispensed</u>."

02. (a) It is an <u>instruction</u> in which we <u>obey</u> Christ.

(b) It is a <u>commemoration</u> in which we <u>remember</u> Christ.

(c) It is a <u>proclamation</u> in which we <u>preach</u> Christ.

(d) It is a <u>participation</u> in which we <u>feed</u> on Christ.

(e) It is an <u>anticipation</u> in which we <u>wait</u> for Christ.

Short Answer

01. two: baptism and the Lord's Supper

02. Catholics believe in transubstantiation, which argues that in Communion, the bread and wine are mysteriously transformed into the literal, physical body and blood of Jesus when they are consumed.

Session 11

Fill in the Blank

01. "Verbal <u>profession</u> minus moral <u>persistence</u> is <u>self-delusion</u>."

02. "Love <u>sees</u> straight. Love <u>thinks</u> clearly. Love <u>frees</u> us from <u>stumbling</u> into unbalanced judgments and conduct."

Short Answer

01. the moral test (obedience) and the social test (love)

02. our growing obedience to God's commands

Session 12

Fill in the Blank

01. "Hospitality is simply <u>opening</u> our doors and <u>allowing</u> people to <u>experience</u> our <u>lives</u> the way they are."

02. "There is nobody in the body of Christ who has not been <u>gifted</u> <u>spiritually</u> under God."

Short Answer

01. prayer, love, hospitality, service, and worship/praise

02. (1) "We have all received spiritual gifts." (2) God "has gifted us in order that we might serve others, not ourselves."

03. "On the basis of the strength which He provides to fulfill the purpose which He intends to engender the praise which He deserves."

Session 13

Fill in the Blank

01. "It is not evangelism—it is not the Gospel—to tell people that there are <u>benefits</u> that attach if they will <u>believe</u> the Gospel. It is not the Gospel to tell people that there are great <u>tragedies</u> that await them if they <u>reject</u> the Gospel."

02. "The <u>Gospel</u> is to tell people who <u>Jesus</u> <u>is</u>, why <u>He</u> <u>came</u>, what <u>He</u> <u>did</u>, why it <u>matters</u>, and that He is the self-proclaimed <u>Savior</u> of the world."

03. Jesus is the only <u>Savior</u> because Jesus is the only one <u>qualified</u> to save.

Short Answer

01. "Passion for reaching people with the Gospel is quenched …. We will find that our zeal for evangelism is diminished."

02. "The unconverted are unaware of the fact of their blindness until God by His grace shows them that they're blind."